SURVIVOR LEGENDS

SURVIVOR LEGENDS

The Players Who Changed the Game

Shaan Merchant

Countryman Press

An Imprint of W. W. Norton & Company
Independent Publishers Since 1923

Jungle art: Teo Tarras / Shutterstock; torch: Herba Mykhailo / iStock Photo

For information about permission to reproduce selections from this book, write to Permissions, Countryman Press, 500 Fifth Avenue, New York, NY 10110

For information about special discounts for bulk purchases, please contact W. W. Norton Special Sales at specialsales@wwnorton.com or 800-233-4830

Manufacturing by Versa Press
Book design by Lovedog Studio
Production manager: Devon Zahn

Countryman Press
www.countrymanpress.com

An imprint of W. W. Norton & Company, Inc.
500 Fifth Avenue, New York, NY 10110
www.wwnorton.com

Authorized EU representative: EAS, Mustamäe tee 50, 10621 Tallinn, Estonia

978-1-324-11216-7

1 2 3 4 5 6 7 8 9 0

To my grandparents: Nani, Nana, Dada, and Ma—
From you, I am me.

"The world, that understandable and lawful world, was slipping away."

—William Golding, *Lord of the Flies*

"We're not bad people. We just play them on TV."

—Kelly Wiglesworth, *Survivor: Borneo*

CONTENTS

CHAPTER 6
Come On In

Introduction:
A Game of Society

ON MAY 31, 2000, MORE THAN 15 MILLION VIEWERS TUNED IN for the premiere of *Survivor*—an astonishing number for a brand-new experiment in reality television. As they clicked their TVs on for this prime-time 8:00 p.m. slot, they saw footage of a group of "ordinary" Americans walking through a small Malaysian fishing village and boarding colorfully painted motorboats that took them to a looming sailing ship in the South China Sea. Over this came the rousing voice of host Jeff Probst:

> *From this tiny Malaysian fishing village, these sixteen Americans are beginning the adventure of a lifetime. They have volunteered to be marooned for thirty-nine days on mysterious Borneo. This is their story. This is* Survivor.

Survivor was a true experiment. CBS primetime audiences were used to seeing the spiritual, sappy soap sagas of *Touched by an Angel,* or a behatted Chuck Norris on *Walker, Texas Ranger.* Now they were being shown a new kind of drama—real people being filmed while they struggled to survive on a remote island. And in this case, survival meant not just building shelter and finding food, but participating in grueling challenges to secure their own safety and maneuvering to vote each other off in a brutal fight for a $1 million prize. It was a wild concept and it would make a big splash.

The impact of the *Survivor* experiment extended past the structure of the show itself and instituted an entirely new genre of television, backed by a major network and made with high-quality production techniques and beautiful cinematography. It was the first significant reality competition show in America. It created the concept of blending documentaries with game shows, plus adding in the high-stakes drama of soap operas by putting real people in a produced setting to duke it out over challenges and melodramatic eliminations. It laid the foundation for one of the most-watched genres of television today: reality TV.

Before *Survivor*, there were a few tentative forays into the reality TV space—in 1973, the PBS documentary series *An American Family* captivated audiences with its *cinema verité* look at the Loud Family. The Loud parents, Pat and Bill, navigated a rocky marriage in California, while one of their sons, Lance Loud, embraced his sexuality in Warholian New York. Despite—or precisely because of—allegations that the filmmakers instigated drama between family members, the series was a smashing success. In 1992, MTV built on this concept by casting a bunch of hot young people to live in an apartment together and be filmed for *The Real World*.

It was in this context that British television producer Charlie Parsons spent over a decade pitching a show concept called *Survive!* to disinterested networks. It was inspired by a Swedish show Parsons sold, *Expedition: Robinson,* as well as by some of his favorite novels: *The Swiss Family Robinson* and *Lord of the Flies*. Parsons was introduced to Mark Burnett, a driven, relentless fellow Brit who was keen on producing a successful adventure show—he had not found success with a 1995 high-octane race concept called *Eco Challenge*. Eventually Parsons sold Burnett the show.[1] The rest is history. Or, rather, the rest is *this* story.

Fifty seasons in, *Survivor* is not just one of the most successful reality shows of all time, but also one of the most influential. It has shaped the genre, and with it, society. Even if you have never

1. Emily Nussbaum's *Cue the Sun* offers a deeper—as well as remarkably researched and incredibly written—look at this history that I highly recommend.

watched an episode of *Survivor*, you have felt its impact: in the format of modern reality TV, with confessionals and eliminations; in the language of alliance and betrayal; in the depiction of "self" as a persona in media; in the shifting ways that society rewards and rejects honesty and duplicity; and in the identity-fracturing elevation of reality figures into full-on celebrity.[2]

Survivor's success launched Burnett into reality TV dominance; he would go on to produce a number of popular franchises including *Are You Smarter than a 5th Grader?*, *Shark Tank*, and *The Voice*. For one of his shows, *The Apprentice*, the search for a drama-ready host led to a brash, tabloid-friendly New York real estate tycoon: Donald Trump. Burnett gave Trump a powerful image rebrand and a weekly national spotlight.[3]

Over the twenty-five years that *Survivor* has played on American televisions, the country around it has changed deeply. The internet era ushered in new stories and more voices, and societal values feel like they are changing at whiplash-inducing speeds. While I wrote and researched this project, I spent my days watching people suffer and starve by choice on *Survivor* while the news showed stories of forced starvation. As I hyperanalyzed duplicitous gameplay on a TV show, ruthlessness has transformed the political culture of this country to a terrifying degree. I hope you read this with the understanding that *Survivor* doesn't exist in a vacuum. It's not a separate entity from the harsh world. *Survivor* is a cultural product made from our world, and shaping it. It is also "just" a game—a fun, sometimes stagy television show made to entertain.

2. The iconic, clichéd phrase of the reality genre, "I'm not here to make friends," even has its origins in *Survivor*'s first season, coined by contestant Kelly Wiglesworth.
3. Trump would return the favor in December of 2024, appointing Burnett to a newly created position as the United States Special Envoy for the United Kingdom.

————

I DON'T QUITE remember if I was one of those 15 million viewers of the *Survivor* premiere. I was only three at the time. But I was certainly among its early viewers, perhaps inappropriately so. For me, *Survivor* began as a family activity on Friday nights—the one day in the week we were allowed to eat dinner in front of the TV. If we forgot to record it (which we almost always did), I'd meet my neighbor at the kitty-corner of our suburban yards for a hand-off of the VHS tape they'd recorded. For over a decade, my family would sit on the sinking beige couch of our family room, with steaming bowls of the day's dinner, and watch the drama of *Survivor* unfold. Today my *Survivor* viewing looks a bit different—VHS tapes are nowhere to be found. I stream the show (ideally live to avoid social media spoilers) typically in my Manhattan apartment, or in Brooklyn bars for watch parties with friends.

Like me, every viewer has their own stories of *Survivor*. Some watched the first few seasons, back when it was appointment viewing for a huge swath of this country, essential for watercooler conversations—and later petered out. In fact, going by the show's viewership ratings, that is the most common experience. Others found *Survivor* during the COVID-19 pandemic, binging season after season with their "COVID pods," watching a campy simulation of society-building while outside, society seemed to be collapsing. With these varied timelines and contexts in which people have come to the show, everyone will naturally have different opinions on the best players and the worst strategies, and on who should be celebrated a hero and who should be scorned a villain.

This book is not an exhaustive list of the people who have made *Survivor* the cultural juggernaut it is today—your favorite players might not be included. More than 750 individuals have competed on the show. Many others have deeply shaped the world we see behind the scenes, from award-winning cinematographers capturing mindblowing shots of nature, to local artisans whittling Immunity Statues.

Instead, this book is a look at the "legends" of *Survivor*, both the lore surrounding the show and the players, those iconic figures who have shaped that lore and become a part of it.

FOR OVER TWO and a half decades, legends have been told and made each week on CBS. But the stunning and dramatic product that ends up on our screens is warped by the layers of lenses used to transform reality into television: the cameras, the edit bay, the producer screenings, the televisions, our own eyes. The show we watch from our couches is polished to tell the story *Survivor*'s creators look to tell, the one that is most exciting or entertaining. But that is just one angle. My hope is to widen the lens.

The chapters that follow are my best attempt to tell the stories of these legends—not just what we saw on screen, but the context behind the camera. I want to explore how the players shape the game, and how the game shaped them.

For this research, I spoke to many former players and surveyed past seasons. I met Richard Hatch at his Rhode Island home; I had coffee with Parvati Shallow and shadowed her on a book tour; I met Sean Rector in his old stomping grounds of Harlem, New York. I had Zoom meetings and phone calls and email correspondence with many of the players and production figures who built these legends and became them.

The players' accounts, in their own words, sometimes confirm and sometimes counter the stories we think we know. This book questions why our opinions of certain players and key moments might be what they are. Who gets to be a hero? Who is deemed a villain? How might the magic of production or the world around us have impacted the opinions we hold? What opinions are shaped by the lens of *Survivor* producers, and when do players take back control of their stories (if that's even possible)?

I didn't speak to every player featured here. You will notice some players' stories include lengthy backgrounds, while some are shorter looks at an immediate impact they made. These stories are told (mostly) chronologically but the themes—the evolution of gameplay, performance, representation—don't always follow those easy lines. Because while these themes are shaped by society, they're ultimately defined by the players—the winners, the juries—and the games they reward. The ultimate focus is the story behind each legend.

Even as *Survivor* continues, seemingly infinitely, the stories I can capture have a limit. I've written this over the summer and fall of 2025. By the time it's published, *Survivor*'s landmark fiftieth season will be airing—and one of these figures profiled may even be its winner.

Fifty seasons in, those fateful words Jeff Probst spoke in 2000 remain true. The logistical details—the number of players participating, the length of the competition—have shifted. There have been new themes and twists each season. But every season still tells the story of "ordinary" strangers marooned together, trying to outwit, outplay, and outlast. This is that story. They are *Survivor*.

How It Works

IF YOU'RE A SEASONED *SURVIVOR* FAN, YOU CAN SAFELY SKIP this page. If you're new—or if it's been a while since you've watched— here's the crash course on the show, so the terms and twists ahead make sense.

At its simplest, *Survivor* strands a group of strangers in a remote location. They build shelter, find food, and compete in challenges. Every few days someone is voted out at **Tribal Council**. The first half of the game is played on teams, called **Tribes.**[4] Midway through the game, the teams come together in the **merge**, and it becomes an individual competition. The final two or three play-ers make their case to the **Jury**—the players voted out since the merge—at a **Final Tribal Council,** and the jury ultimately votes for one winner.

Survivor has invented its own language over the years, so there are some key terms to know:

Tribes: The starting teams
Castaways: A word for all of the players

---

4. With the use of this word, and in many of the themes, sounds, and styles, *Survivor* has borrowed liberally from a collage of Indigenous and global motifs—a kind of pop-culture orientalism that appropriates from many non-Western cultures to create a sense of the "exotic" and dangerous. I won't be going into this deeply in the book, but it must be acknowledged.

Tribal Council: A torch-lit assembly during which the players review the past days by answering probing questions from Jeff Probst, then ultimately cast their vote by writing it on a parchment and putting it into an urn. Once the votes are read, Probst snuffs the torch of the player eliminated.

Confessional: While technically an interview with producers, this is the "talking head" analysis of the game by the players; a format that revolutionized the industry.

Merge: The moment, typically marked by Jeff Probst announcing "drop your buffs" and a celebratory feast, at which the tribes are combined and the game becomes individual.

Jury: The players voted out after the merge who watch Tribal Council and ultimately vote for a winner.

Immunity: Safety; the golden ticket. During the team portion of the game, only the losing team goes to Tribal Council to eliminate a player. The winning team receives an **Immunity Statue**. After the merge, the single winning player receives an **Immunity Necklace** marking their safety.

Hidden Immunity Idol: A hidden token buried in the game. The finder can try to keep it secret. If you find it, you can play it once after the votes are cast but typically before they're read, to save yourself or an ally.

Final Tribal Council: The climax. The jury questions the finalists and votes to award the million dollars and title of Sole Survivor.

CHAPTER 1

Original Sin

The Birth of the Game

Richard Hatch
& Sue Hawk

ON MARCH 13, 2000, SIXTEEN AMERICANS MADE THEIR WAY through a fishing village on stilts over the South China Sea. They had flown from around the country to Malaysia—Borneo—having gone through an extensive casting process and agreeing to participate in this unique television experiment—to be filmed while trying to survive on a remote jungle island for thirty-nine days, simultaneously voting to kick each other off the island. Now, after months of prep and interviews and uncertainty, it was happening. The cameras were rolling.

One of the people walking through that village was a thirty-nine-year-old corporate trainer from Newport, Rhode Island, **Richard Hatch.** His mind was racing: "Who are the people living here on posts above the water? Abject poverty doesn't even begin to describe it. And yet we're here with this camera crew filming these white people walking through. What the fuck? Oh wait, the game, the game, the game . . . Who are these other people, why are we in these groups? Is this my team?"

As he tried to process everything happening around him, the players were shepherded onto motorboats and arrived at a looming ship with big black sails. On the ship was a fresh-faced, dimple-cheeked Jeff Probst, the host. Then, it happened fast. Jeff explained that they had two minutes to throw over their bamboo rafts, oars, and whatever supplies they could from the ship before paddling to their respective camps, small islands—that little point there in the horizon. Now, "Go!"

The game had started. These strangers scrambled, grabbing nets and rope and knives and bags of rice, then they jumped off the ship into the open ocean, and began a grueling, hours-long paddle to their beachy outposts on the Pulau Tiga islands of Borneo.

As Richard's Tagi Tribe finally made it to their assigned beach, exhausted, they set out to figure out what was next. They had gotten themselves to this island; now they had to survive for thirty-nine days. They evaluated their next steps, talking over each other in anxious, excited voices: they needed shelter, to find a water source, to build a latrine. It was only day one of thirty-nine—did they need to build a fire already?

Richard sat quietly, back against a tree, shirtless, watching. He had a rounded stomach, scruffy stubble and observant blue eyes, darting back and forth. Then he piped up, "I think the first thing we need to do is talk about whatever we're going to do, talk about the process." Rudy Boesch, a curmudgeonly seventy-two-year-old former Navy SEAL, responded swiftly and with authority: The plan was to build the shelter, then the latrine further down. Overtalk continued as everyone headed out to try to do something helpful. But Richard wasn't satisfied.

"I think we're off to a bad start," he told Sue Hawk, a Wisconsin truck driver with a thick midwestern accent. She pushed back—she's a self-described "redneck" and in her world, you work as you talk—in this case, you chat while you build the shelter. Richard agreed, the work was important, but he sensed something about this experience that other contestants hadn't. This was the pilot episode, and beyond survival there was no blueprint for how to play this bizarre new game with cameras. They needed to sort out the big picture of this televised experiment: "Why are we here? What's the point?"

Richard wanted to set a tone. He was curious about his teammates, wanting to understand their philosophies and how they planned to navigate this new experience. He wanted to communicate and strategize, but his tribe was preoccupied with the basics: gathering wood and making small talk.

Richard was there for one reason: to win the million-dollar prize. In his very first confessional to the cameras, he said: "I'm good to go survival-wise. People-wise, it'll be a little more challenging.

But I've got the million-dollar check written already. I mean, I'm the winner."

He was confident, but he was right. Richard Hatch became the first winner of *Survivor*. He invented the playbook for reality competition strategy, and in doing so became America's first reality TV villain.

Twenty-five years later I met with Richard, sitting by the modest pool of his Newport, Rhode Island, home as his four squat mutts waddled around. We discussed his *Survivor* story—the many ways it made a lasting impact on him and the many ways he made a lasting impact on it.

RICHARD HATCH GREW up in Newport, a charming New England beach town. He drove me past the rocky shores he dove from to spear fish—a skill that would become essential to his *Survivor* game—and his grandmother's home where he would go for holiday visits. But Richard's early life wasn't easy. He was raped when he was eight, molested when he was ten, and his thirteen-year-old brother was run over and killed when Richard was fifteen.

Richard didn't feel supported or understood by his parents, who divorced. He described his mom as "very superficial and private." His lasting memory of his dad, a lobsterman and cop, is of "him in his underwear, my mother just yelling at him all the time, 'get another job.'" Richard, who is gay, recalls regularly hearing slurs used around the home.

This childhood made Hatch a thinker. "There was a lot of, *What is going on in that head?*" He's analytical and likes to figure people out. It's another skill that made him a strong *Survivor* player.

Eager to leave home, Richard dropped out of high school his senior year. But a physics teacher at his school, Paul Mello, saw something in him. He found Richard "in a bar or whatever" and told him he was too bright to not graduate. Mello let Richard live with him, driving him into school every morning and finding him a job painting houses. He also invited Richard to an outdoor education program he had founded in Maine, Horizon Bound. "He took half 'troubled teens' and half 'regular teens.' I was supposedly a regular teen," Hatch says with a knowing chuckle.

The outdoor experience was life-changing. "Oh fuck, you have no idea, life altering. That month did exactly what he knew it would do for me." Richard learned to communicate, to work with others for survival, and to be introspective. "It just shakes it all up in a way that exposes you to yourself."

After graduating, Hatch bounced around careers: He went to college in Florida to study marine biology. He went to West Point and served in the Army. He ran a Bugle Boy retail store and managed a grocery store. He did "corporate training," which is how he's introduced on the show. Throughout all of this, Richard found time to be outdoors: climbing mountains around the country, hiking, canoeing, diving.

He first learned about *Survivor*—or at least, the concept of *Survivor*—on the phone with his mom, Peggy. She had seen an advertisement for casting and called him: "She said, 'Hey, they're putting together a show made for you,'" but she didn't remember the channel or any of the details. He was kind of like, "Great, ma. Thanks." But a week later, another friend called him with the same message: "They're doing this show, it's literally made for you." "I said, 'What the fuck are you doing? Did you talk to Peggy?'" No, this friend had seen it too, and she remembered the details, so Richard looked it up. "She was right." He would have paid to go on outdoor adventures like this in the wilderness; the gameplay would come easily too.

RICHARD PRINTED OUT the application, recognizing he had to be interesting—"Who would you not want to be stuck on the island with?"—"Morons and bigots and bores, oh my!" It was enough to get him an interview.

In his interviews, Richard played up his ego and confidence. "I wasn't just me; I was me beyond, me on steroids." He understood that production was looking to cast good TV characters, and that meant playing it up. Hatch remembers going into one of the final interviews, where he found twenty to thirty CBS executives—"the decision makers"—sitting in a semicircle with an empty chair in the middle. He walked in confidently, but he didn't sit down. "I put my hand on the chair and I said, 'Listen, you know you're gonna pick me. What you don't know is I'm gonna win and what you need to know for planning purposes, I'm gonna host next year's show.'" He walked out to them laughing.

Production did cast him and he did win. He thinks they expected the other players would find his confidence grating, and assumed he would be the first person voted off. But in the same way he knew he had to play up his ego in the casting process, he knew that living with fifteen big-personality strangers on a beach for thirty-nine days would require the opposite, so he turned it down—at least a bit.

This persona creation and strategy around self-presentation may seem obvious today, in the age of social media when everyone is presenting a distorted version of themselves, refracted through the lens of our now-ubiquitous screens. But this was the early days of reality TV, pre-Instagram. Richard Hatch was building the now-obvious concept of a media persona. He understood that even though survival was an essential part of the show, an equally important factor was *performance*.

Casting director Lynne Spillman remembers seeing Richard sitting in the lobby of the Santa Monica, California hotel where the interviews took place, watching people, and taking notes. She says she now sees that he was playing *Survivor* before many on production even fully understood the strategy and analysis the game would require.

(continued)

Spillman—whose insights you'll hear throughout this book—was the genius who cast most of these legendary players (though she is always quick to remind, casting is a big team. She calls her best skillset "hiring the right people").

Lynne began her career in fashion in New York, as a buyer. After several years of the grind, she was ready for a break. She moved to California, eager to take the summer off, but at her first dinner out with friends, one was impressed by her. "You're going to come work with me on Monday," he told her. Spillman said no, but the next day, he was at her house, ready to pick her up for work. "I guess I'm doing this," she figured. Lynne was officially working for MTV, originally answering phones until it became clear she had a knack for people. She had grown up traveling, and went to camp with people from all over the country. She loved having "a good sense of what people are like, around the country."

Spillman began casting for *Singled Out*, an MTV dating game show. She had to find fifty men and fifty women every day: "We were hustling. It was hard." Spillman was at the forefront of this niche "real people casting." After a few years of that hustle in the mid to late 1990s, Spillman was pregnant and again ready for that break she never got when she received a call from Mark Burnett about a new show he was casting for. She told him, "I'll meet with you, but I'm not going to do it." Then she saw "thirty seconds on a VHS tape" of the concept and realized, "I have to do this." She saw that *Survivor* would be "something different, something special." Her husband told her, "Negotiate like a man." Spillman handed Burnett a paper with her requests—he agreed. Spillman would lead casting for *Survivor*.

She remembers the uncertainty of those early days. "I didn't even know what I was casting." She called Burnett, "Are they going to be swimming? Do they need to know how to?" "Oh, good question. I guess." The assignment was to "think of it like a shipwreck." People from all walks of life, who might never meet otherwise. As tapes came in, Lynne and her team sat in the office kitchen, using the refrigerator as a casting board, putting up the pictures of the players they liked. "I could start picturing the relationships." It was through this process that they found their cast—Richard and Rudy and Sue, the innocent student Colleen Haskell, and the iconically irreverent Greg Buis. Once her part of the job was done, Spillman remembers watching the first episode. "It was the most beautiful TV that had ever aired," she says. "You knew you were making history when you saw the first episode."

Spillman helped find the characters that made *Survivor* a hit. For the first season, they had around two thousand applicants. By the second season, they had seventy thousand. And for the next thirty-nine seasons, she would lead the team that found the players that shaped this game.

WHEN RICHARD ARRIVED on that hot Tagi beach after the arduous row in, he was already thinking about how to win—to perform and strategize. But his tribemates rushing off to gather shelter materials suggested to him now wasn't the time to talk strategy. So, he had to adapt. Hatch hunkered down and worked hard to be a provider. "The guy surprises me," the Navy vet Rudy explained. "You know, he's fat, but he's good." Richard used those spear fishing skills, honed on the Newport coast, to become an essential to his tribe. "Keep me, I'm getting the fish," he told his tribemates early on. Meanwhile, to the camera: "I'm planning something different . . . and it's a little sneaky."

The fact that while trying to get to know each other and survive the contestants had to eliminate each other, vote someone off the island, was difficult. Most players focused on practicality. The first castaway eliminated was the sixty-three-year-old musician, Sonja Christopher, who had stumbled at a challenge causing the loss. At Tribal Council, players made undiscussed decisions, most of them focused on eliminating players based on strength, work ethic, or interpersonal clashes. One player, neurologist Sean Kenniff, even voted alphabetically in an attempt to avoid moral conflict. Most didn't yet understand, or accept, that "gameplay" went beyond survival and challenges. It would be psychological, and social. Eliminating your fellow society-builders would require some ruthlessness.

Richard saw the bigger picture: Winning this game would take *strategy*.

"I . . . wanted to talk with the group about who we were voting for before . . . but boy did that not fly," he told producers in an Episode 3 confessional. It is hard to imagine today, when over half of a *Survivor* episode focuses on strategic conversations around who to eliminate. But at the time, there were no visible strategy discussions on the show. "They were not counting votes, they were thinking let's play honestly, vote your conscience," Hatch says. "I don't get the point of that . . . It's a game with rules: outwit, outplay, outlast. Well, that's not outwitting."

To gain control, Richard had an idea that would shape reality television forever: an alliance. This would be a loyal group who would vote together and, with the power of their numerical advantage, advance to the end of the competition.

He first approached Rudy.[5] To the producers' potential dismay, Richard had earned Rudy's respect, "For a homosexual, he's one of the nicest guys I ever met. And he's good at what he does . . . Me and Richard got to be pretty good friends—not in a homosexual way, that's for sure." Still, Rudy resisted the idea of an alliance, questioning the ethics of teaming up. "I couldn't even imagine [an

5. Richard believes he and Rudy were put on the same tribe to spark conflict: "the gay, naked Army guy versus the older, traditional Navy guy."

alliance] was something problematic until Rudy wasn't willing," Richard says now.

So he pivoted, pitching the idea to the Wisconsin trucker Sue and twenty-two-year-old rafting instructor Kelly Wiglesworth. "We really could control our fate if we stick together," Sue realized. Eventually, Rudy joined too. "I don't agree with his lifestyle, and he probably don't agree with mine, but anyway, we gotta work together." With that, *Survivor*'s first alliance—the Tagi Four—was born.

Perhaps the best example of the power of this alliance can be seen in the first elimination after the merge, when the two tribes became one. All the other players voted "their conscience," individually and differently. The Tagi Four planned their vote together, targeting Air Force Survival Instructor Gretchen Cordy, who was seen as the leader of the opposing Pagong tribe. She was eliminated in a 1-1-1-1-1-1-4 vote. "Oh my god, it's me," she realized, in shock, as Jeff read the final four parchments, all with her name written on them—*Survivor*'s first blindside.

Hatch invented the first alliance. Today, that concept is part of the reality genre's lingua franca. But at the time, their essential nature wasn't understood. He reframed the whole premise: This wasn't just about how well you could survive the wilderness; it was about how well you could survive each other. That shift didn't just change *Survivor*; it planted the DNA for all reality competition shows that followed.

Castaways—and later, viewers—grappled with whether it was fair to play this way, to "gang up" and manipulate the game in your favor. Kelly Wiglesworth struggled with her role in the alliance: "How do you stay true to yourself and maintain integrity and still play this game?" she asked. Later, she reconciled: "We're not bad people. We just play them on TV." It was one of the first recognitions that playing this game for a million dollars might mean becoming someone slightly different on screen—doing things you wouldn't in the "real world." In other words, there was already a sense of performance and strategizing baked into this expression of reality.

Colleen Haskell, a college student who became known as "America's Sweetheart" and went on to a short-lived acting career following her time on the show, was appalled: "They're outright lying on national television! . . . Is a deserving person going to win this money? The answer to that question is no." This tension between authenticity and performance was new for the players, trying to understand how to present themselves. It was equally new to audiences too, who weren't yet used to watching "real people" filtered through their television screens.

To Richard, there was never any dilemma about his approach. "A football player doesn't tap his opponent on his shoulder and say, 'Hey, I'm about to tackle you.' He fucking plows him," he says. He wasn't worried about seeming like the best person—it was about playing the best game. Through his time on the show, Richard determined those unwritten rules—manipulation and strategy are not just acceptable, but essential in reality competition—and ultimately he opened a Pandora's Box that would shape the genre and his life. But in 2000, in the eyes of a traditional and uncertain CBS audience, that boldness made him objectionable.

ONE BY ONE, the Tagi Four eliminated every other player from the rival Pagong tribe, and then the non-aligned players from their own. Since, "Pagong-ing" has become the term for the systematic elimination of another tribe or group by an alliance in power.

When just the Tagi Four remained, trucker Sue was the first to be eliminated. The remaining three were left to compete in the final challenge of the game, Hands on a Hard Idol, and it showed the depth of Rich's analysis.

The challenge was one of pure willpower. The contestants, standing on a tree stump, simply had to leave their hands on an Immunity Statue. The person who kept in contact the longest would win, guaranteeing their spot in the finale and granting them the choice of which player to bring as their final competitor.

Richard, Rudy, and Kelly stood in the Borneo heat with their arms outstretched. Richard considered his options, running through each scenario in his head just as he had since day one.

If he won, he would secure his spot at Final Tribal Council, but have to make the difficult decision of who to eliminate and who to take to the finale with him. Early on, he had made a pact with Rudy to get to the end together, but he also knew that Rudy was beloved by the jury and it would be difficult to win votes against him. If he brought Kelly, he would be seen as going back on his word with Rudy—the one relationship he was true to throughout—and likely lose any remaining goodwill the jury had for him. Losing, strangely, seemed safer: If Rudy won, Richard trusted that he would stay loyal to their pact. If Kelly won, it was likely she might also recognize she had a better chance of beating Richard than Rudy. Hatch's best chance at winning the war, he realized, might just be losing this battle.

But after thirty-eight days of exhaustion, another voice crept in: Was he self-sabotaging? He thought back through his life, of the self-love he struggled so hard to build and of which he was still constantly needing to remind himself. Was he giving up? Was this move him undercutting all the hard work he did to get here, or was he making the ultimate strategic decision? After two and a half hours, he made his choice: He took his hand off first, quitting the challenge.

THE FINALE OF *Survivor*'s first season was watched by an estimated 51.7 million people. It remains the most-watched episode of the show ever, and was the second most-watched televised event of the year 2000 after only the Super Bowl. More people watched *Survivor* than The Oscars, the World Series or any episode of any television series in the 2000s, other than the finale of *Friends*. And after it aired, the topic of many watercooler conversations was **Sue Hawk**. Sue cemented her legacy with a stunning speech during Final Tribal Council—known in *Survivor* lore as the "Snakes and Rats" speech—and became the show's first bitter juror.

Sue, the Wisconsin truck driver, played *Survivor* with an open mind, open heart, and open mouth. She worked hard and approached the game with gumption and bluntness, embodying her "we work as we talk" ethos.

Sue supported the idea of an alliance from the get-go; they were already everywhere in society. "America is run on alliances. The minute somebody gives money to the president for his campaign as a lobbyist, that's an alliance . . . Same thing when people go [to] the church, and they're not religious, but . . . maybe they're an insurance agent and wanna sell more insurance in town, or they're a real estate agent and they wanna sell real estates and they wanna meet up with people. So there's gonna be an alliance. Don't tell me there ain't alliances." The conspiring that many players saw as unseemly in the *Survivor* society they were building, Sue recognized as a very real part of society outside of the game.

Sue seemed to understand the game in a way unmatched by any player except Richard Hatch. And she was ready to turn on him. "My strategy all along has been to play the role of dumb redneck. People think rednecks are so vulnerable and dumb. They'll talk to 'em openly . . . Hopefully in the end, the old redneck will burn the city slicker," she said. Her relationship with Richard was based in gameplay, but she was making very real connections in the game too.

Sue built a deep friendship with Kelly Wiglesworth—and their relationship appeared to go beyond just the game and their alliance. "Right now I don't trust anybody except for Kelly. I trust Kelly 100 percent," Sue said. She shared that she lost her best friend twenty years prior, and that in Kelly, for the first time, she found someone she could open up to again. "I ain't gonna fuck her. I'm not burning her," she added, the rough trucker's voice quivering near tears for the first time in a confessional. It is one of those emotionally resonant moments where the game and life intertwine—as much as there's a game to be played, there are real relationships being formed and feelings at stake. This has become one of the central tensions of *Survivor*: How do you play a cutthroat game against people you have grown to love? Kelly and Sue were the first players to explore those muddy waters.

But a duo that strong became a liability. When Richard noticed Sue was wary of Kelly spending time with the other, younger women from the Pagong tribe after the merge, he decided to pounce on that insecurity—to widen that budding rift by reinforcing that, yes, it does look like she's playing both sides.

Their once ironclad friendship unraveled dramatically over the final episodes, with Sue losing her trust in Kelly. But for Richard, that unraveling came right on time.

It all came to a head at the final four, when the once-aligned Tagi had to turn on one of their own. Kelly had immunity; she was safe. Jeff read the votes: one for Sue, one for Richard, another for Sue, another for Richard—the first tie in *Survivor* history. Richard and Rudy had targeted Sue, while Sue and Kelly had gone for Richard. Now Kelly and Rudy had to revote.

At the booth, Kelly lingered over her parchment. Would she cut her former friend, or the alliance leader who got them this far? Finally, with a weary shrug, she wrote a name onto the parchment. The votes were read. First vote: Sue. Second vote: Sue. Kelly voted out her once-great friend. Sue grabbed her torch in hand, half-giggling in disbelief. Jeff snuffed it. "The tribe has spoken."

Kelly ended up winning the final Hands on a Hard Idol challenge that Hatch quit and, just as he predicted, she chose to eliminate Rudy and bring Richard to the finals. While making her case to the jury, Kelly asked to be judged not by how she played the game, but by the person she is. Richard took the opposite approach, owning his game as one of strategy all along; he hoped the better gameplayer, not the better person, would win. The jury had to decide what kind of game they would reward. Would it be Kelly's appeal to personal character, or Richard's unapologetic embrace of strategy?

One by one, the jury asked questions to help guide their decision. When it came time for Sue to speak, her tone had changed. She walked to the front, slowly, the firelight from the torches reflecting in her eyes. Then, she gave what would become one of the most iconic monologues in reality TV history. With her steadfast bluntness she looked at Kelly: "If I were ever to pass you in this life again, and you were laying there, dying of thirst, I would not give you a drink of water. I'd just let the vultures take you, and do whatever they want with you, with no ill regrets." Then, turning to the jury, she "pleaded" they consider the spirit of the island they had played on when making their decision. An island full of only two things—snakes and rats:

We have Richard the snake, who knowingly went after prey; and Kelly, who turned into the rat that ran around like the rats do on this island, trying to run from the snake. And I feel we owe it to the island's spirit that we have learned to come to know, to let it be, in the end, the way Mother Nature intended it to be: for the Snake to eat the Rat.

Sue voted for Richard. It was the deciding vote, and he won 4-3. Sue helped make *Survivor* must-watch television with her theatrics, but also placed the vote that decided what type of game would be accepted. The snakes would eat the rats. Snakes would win *Survivor*.

Sue and Richard's paths would cross again, in unfortunate circumstances, seven seasons later when both returned for *Survivor: All-Stars*. During a challenge on a balance beam, Richard was playing naked. He and Sue were talking smack when she turned around to pass him. As they maneuvered on the tight platform, Sue says Richard thrust his groin at her. Richard was—unrelatedly—eliminated that night. The next day, Sue quit the game, saying she felt violated. Richard says he wasn't told about this, and only learned about her feelings on the incident right before the season aired. Both parties met with a mediator and CBS. Sue did not press charges against Hatch, CBS, or Burnett. She and Richard appeared together on *The Early Show* the day following the episode airing where Sue said they "agreed to move forward and past it."

AFTER WINNING, RICHARD says he felt pride in himself in a way he never had before, "and that was pretty powerful. I had gotten to a place where I loved me, playing this game." He was never the golden child, never the sports star, but on *Survivor*, he was the MVP. He played it the best, and he came out on top.

Richard waited eagerly for the show to air, not even telling his family he had won. "People are actually going to see me now," he thought. "They're gonna get it. They're going to see how sharp I am."

Then the show aired.

"Wow, how wrong was I?" he says, now.

This was the first time Richard miscalculated. He expected recognition as a brilliant strategist—but instead became America's most prominent TV villain. Even before social media was there to amplify every cruel thought anyone had, the backlash to Richard Hatch in 2000 came fast and loud, ringing through every facet of media at the time: David Letterman mocked him as "the naked fat guy," and said there should be riots on the street if he won. Rosie O'Donnell had the players on her show and gifted all the others new cars while handing Richard a bag of rice (the only food they had on the island). Tabloids put out gossip about Richard and his son. Newspapers and magazine critics branded him "evil" and "manipulative" ("'Machiavellian' I didn't really mind," Richard says). He received death threats in the mail and jeers on the streets.

"They didn't get it," Richard says. He thought people would see how sharp he was, but instead he became the target of America's first mass backlash against a new kind of celebrity. The ire wasn't directed toward a politician or actor caught in a scandal, or even toward a possibly murderous sports star, but toward a real person, who had appeared on TV as himself and played a game. It's left a pain that Hatch bats away with quick jokes or frustrated tangents, but one anyone would still feel deeply.

To many Americans at the time, there was something immoral about Richard. Part of that was how he played the game, his strategizing and scheming, but part of that could have also been who he was. Richard was often nude around camp, a choice he says was about comfort, freedom, and even strategy—it was hot, clothes got wet, and cameramen (at that time, all men) avoided following his "hairy ass," giving him privacy. He also wanted to challenge America's "puritanical mindset."

He was also openly gay and openly atheist. Richard says had many meaningful on-screen conversations about both with Rudy and bible-toting dairy farmer Dirk Been. But viewers "heard very few of the conversations that I think might have been most impactful," he says. "Later I understood why: 'Cause the producers have their own limits and intentions and ideas about how they wanted people to be impacted."

The villain edit and reception he received wasn't promoted by his tribemates while filming. Despite their qualms with his strategic gameplay, Richard was called "such a sweetheart," "so easy-going," and "the gay compassionate guy" on-air. Villainousness certainly wasn't the impression I got from the warm and reflective person I met twenty-five years later.

But in both the game of *Survivor* and in this game we call society, viewers need characters to root for and against. For the latter, producers and audience members alike need look no further than the gay, naked atheist who was eager to strategize and willing to manipulate. In the years to come, *Survivor* villains would become fan-favorites, celebrated for their entertainment value and deviousness, but pioneers like Hatch didn't get that reception.

Richard is proud of his game. He often hears from LGBTQ fans about how much his open visibility meant to them. But the weight of the negativity "crushed" him, he says. "I convinced myself, 'Oh well.' But the impact was horribly negative."

It was the first time anyone had to navigate life after being cast as a reality TV villain, and there was no playbook and no support for that. Richard feels *Survivor* leadership has never reckoned with that impact. "I have great respect for [Jeff Probst's] role as a host, but I don't respect his failure to take responsibility for the power that he has and the way in which he wields it without accounting for his own biases." After the first season ended, the show's executive producer Mark Burnett told him they were "family now." But when Richard asked for support, he never got it.

The show impacted Hatch's life in another major way. He says there was confusion about who owed what taxes on his prize money—what was owed to the Malaysian government versus the US government, what production was paying and what he was responsible for. This was all so new for the cast and production alike.

In September of 2005, he was indicted by a federal grand jury on charges of tax evasion and sentenced to fifty-one months in prison the following year. He was released in 2009, then later served another nine months in 2011 for violation of his release terms by failing to amend his returns. He says he is still dealing with the legal fallout to this day. The headlines reinforced his image as a schemer.

"I don't have animosity or anger toward [Probst and Burnett], but I have disappointment beyond what I could possibly communicate," Richard says. "They are in these privileged positions and have watched for twenty-five years without ever checking in to see how they have affected and caused much of this devastation in my life."

Legally, Richard erred and was found guilty by the court of law. Culturally, he faced the wrath of the court of public opinion. But it's hard not to see how the way his *Survivor* story was told might have shaped how his post-*Survivor* story unfolded. He was America's most-watched TV villain—and the first to have to survive what that meant when the cameras turned off.

———

THERE'S ANOTHER WAY Hatch's *Survivor* story might have been told: He was a troubled but bright child who found himself and built his confidence in the outdoors. He learned about *Survivor* because multiple people in his life, the people who knew him best, told him it was a show that was *made for him*. And it was—he thrived in the outdoors and provided for his team, he built the first alliance, brought strategy to the forefront, and created the space for entertainment and opinions. He made *Survivor* the game it is today—he knew how to be a character and understood the strategy needed to win before its top brass even did.

Just three years after Ellen DeGeneres came out on national television and two years after Matthew Shepard was brutally tortured and left to die in Laramie, Wyoming, the face of America's most-watched television show was an openly gay Army veteran whose closest ally was a grumbling, homophobic Navy SEAL. They respected each other as human beings, looking past their differences to work toward a common goal. "There's so much more we could have done with that relationship," Hatch says. There's so much more that could have been done with his story.

I ask Richard if he regrets doing *Survivor*. For the first time in our conversation, he hesitates. "I don't know if I can really answer that," he says, "It's a great game." He still watches every episode to this day. "I can't say I regret it. I regret who we are as humans that have enabled this incredible experience that could have been so positive to be as negative as it was."

Richard Hatch changed the trajectory of television. He built the blueprint for how this strange new experiment could be won—and in the process became its cautionary tale. He showed what it takes to outwit, outplay, and outlast, and revealed what it costs to do so. Ultimately, the impact of those things may just be more costly than the million-dollar check for which he fought so hard.

Colby Donaldson, Tina Wesson & Jerri Manthey

SURVIVOR FOUND ITS VILLAIN IN SEASON 1. BY SEASON 2, IT had found its "hero."

Colby Donaldson was a strapping Texan who loved his mama, had a strong work ethic and a relentless competitive drive. "When I wake up, there's two things I'm thankful for: I'm thankful I'm alive and I'm thankful I'm a Texan," he said in one of his first confessionals.

Season 2, set in the Australian Outback, opens with a 5-mile trek through the deep sands of the Herbert River region, with contestants hauling any supplies they might need. Colby, as the young muscle of the team, was carrying more weight than anyone else, he reminded viewers, but added that he loved the intensity of the trek. "It fires me up and shows me what people are made of."

"The Colbster," as he sometimes referred to himself, was the whole package: He had movie-star looks; he was kind and gentlemanly (well, mostly—see Jerri Manthey, page 34); and he was a challenge powerhouse. He won five individual Immunity Challenges, a record (since tied) that still stands.

But his true impact wasn't in his gameplay, but his character. Colby became *Survivor*'s first archetypal hero—clean-cut, chivalrous, and deeply American at a time when the country was eager for uncomplicated icons. In 2001, as reality TV was still proving itself to mainstream audiences, Colby embodied what producers believed America wanted to root for: strength without scheming, charm without cynicism. His popularity proved them right. According to the Baby Name Institute, the name "Colby" jumped 166 percent in 2001—over 2,000 more children were named Colby after his *Survivor* appearance—and he parlayed his fame into a TV hosting career. He was, as Jeff Probst called him, "*Survivor*'s first All-American Hero," though he wasn't a fireman or a veteran and never saved kittens from a burning building—he worked as an auto customizer. Still, he established a character blueprint the show would try to recreate for years.

The defining moment of Colby's game came when he won the final Immunity Challenge and chose to bring the beloved mother of two, Tina Wesson, to the Final Tribal Council instead of Keith Famie, an aloof chef who had alienated several jurors. Many saw Colby's decision as noble, others saw it as foolish. Ultimately, it may have cost him $1 million.

TINA WESSON WON *Survivor: Australian Outback*, and in many ways she was the true hero of the season that may have ultimately saved the show.

After Richard Hatch's win, producers worried that *Survivor* was in trouble. "We thought it was the end of the show: The big naked evil villain wins," Jeff Probst said in a 2018 interview. Colby may have been the hero they built up, but **Tina Wesson** was the one who quietly got the job done. She was deeply strategic, but proved that strategy didn't have to be equated with ruthlessness.

The forty-year-old East Tennessee native never wanted to be in front of the camera: "I barely like being in front of other people," she tells me, but her husband encouraged her to apply given her athletic ability and love of the outdoors—she still lives rurally. After casting interviews in Philadelphia and Los Angeles, Tina got the call: She hadn't made the cut. They were going with someone else to fulfill the "soccer mom" archetype. But a few days later, another call came in. "They said the girl they had asked said, 'Let me think about it,' and Mark Burnett said, 'I don't want anyone who has to think about it. Call Tina.'"

I ask Tina what she thinks sealed the deal for her casting: "I would say partly it's my accent," adding cheekily, "not that I have an accent," in her Tennessee twang.

In the first several episodes of Season 2, Tina was hidden—sometimes literally, behind Colby's bulging biceps. She had entered *Survivor* with a plan: She wanted to have "an all-nice alliance." She wanted to play with people who wanted to "do good" with the money and to "never say anything negative about anybody." She respects Richard Hatch—who is now a friend—and gives him credit for creating the "alliance mentality." But as a viewer, she admits, it was "kind of brutal" to watch that first season and not want any of the finalists to win.

But, as it goes on *Survivor*, Tina had to adapt. In the opening minutes, as they made that trek to the camp, Tina says Mitchell Olson, a South Dakotan singer/songwriter approached her. He had learned from watching the dynamics of the first season, and was building an alliance right now—was she in or was she out? She figured it was better to be part of it than not. "So, ten minutes off the plane, it was already Plan B," she says. Tina went along with Mitchell's quickly formed alliance for a few days, until the chef, Keith Famie, was on the chopping block. She noticed a theme in the eliminations: The older players were being targeted. She might be next.

So, on the long walk to Tribal Council that night, Tina approached Keith and Colby, offering Keith a lifeline and convincing Colby to flip; they would vote for Mitchell instead. Tina orchestrated what is arguably the first flip against an alliance in *Survivor* history, but there was a problem. With these conversations happening in transit, when the contestants weren't being filmed, there was no footage—no way to tell this story on screen. Not only did this missing moment lead to Tina being underrated as a strategist, but it also shaped the show's production going forward. Since Season 2, contestants are put "on lockdown" during all travel and transitions, required to stay silent while the cameras aren't running.

Colby and Tina's relationship grew: An alliance, yes, but also a natural kinship born out of a respect for their mutual competitive, athletic spirit and the Southern charm they both brought to the game. It showed a different kind of alliance could be created—their bond was more about shared values and mutual respect than cold calculation. Keith rounded out this alliance of three.

Just before the merge, a member of the opposing Kucha tribe fell into their fire and had to be medevacked out of the game. It was one of those sobering reminders of just how dangerous *Survivor* can be.

Because of this, both tribes entered the merge with an even number of contestants. Having learned their lessons from the chaotic individual voting last season, each tribe came determined to vote together. This was already a different game, thanks to Richard Hatch.

The first challenge after the merge was simple: stand on a platform in the water for as long as you can. Jeff Probst brought out treats to tempt the starving players off their stands—peanut butter and chocolate, ice cream, coffee. Many were tempted and jumped. Tina did not.

Over ten hours in, only Tina and Keith remained. As she stood shivering above the dark waters, Tina was thinking ahead to Tribal Council. She remembered a tricky rule: In the event of a tie, this season, the tiebreaker would go to the player with fewer previous votes. Tina had never received any, while Keith had collected several earlier in the game (from when she orchestrated the flip on Mitchell). If the opposing Kucha tribe voted together for Keith, she assumed he would lose the tiebreaker while she and her other tribemates could survive it. So, after ten hours of standing still and resisting every delicious offer, she stepped off, letting Keith win immunity.

At Tribal, Tina's Ogakor tribe voted for Kucha's Jeff Varner, who had received previous votes. With Keith safe under the protection of the Immunity Necklace, the Kucha tribe members voted for Colby, whose name had yet to be written down. The tie meant Varner was eliminated. Tina had quietly secured control of the game for her alliance. With this power in numbers, they steadily eliminated every other player and reached the final three.

"I so, so wish I had won that final challenge," says Tina. It wasn't one of pure muscle power—though she was a tough competitor in those too—but one that played to her strength as a relational, social player: trivia about her former tribemates. She and Colby were tied going into Jeff's last question, "Who listed their proudest accomplishment as being on the Dean's List in college?" "It was just one of those things where I guess Amber and Colby had that conversation and I hadn't," Tina says. She answered incorrectly and Colby won immunity, making that fateful decision to take her to the end. "He took me because we had a pact," Tina says. Had she won, she would have done the same, and perhaps the public discourse around the game would have been different. Colby wouldn't have had to endure the criticism he got for that decision, with "people saying he was just a Mama's boy," and that story wouldn't have overshadowed Tina's impressive win.

Tina returned for Season 8's *All-Stars,* but was the first player voted out, with previous winners being targeted from the outset. She played again alongside her daughter, Katie, in *Survivor: Blood vs. Water,* the twenty-seventh season. Even a decade later, she played with the same social savvy and athletic prowess. She was voted out shortly after the merge, but this season employed a *Redemption Island* twist, in which eliminated players would compete in duels for an eventual chance to reenter the game. She showed off her physical ability by surviving through four duels, then winning the fifth to earn her way back. But she was quickly eliminated again right before the finale—this time for good—given her high likelihood to win again.

Tina considers herself "the most ordinary person in the world." But through her kindness and adaptable gameplay, she quietly reshaped *Survivor*'s trajectory. She had seen, and felt, the distaste of Richard Hatch's win—for *Survivor* as a cutthroat battle of wits. She brought wits too, and played a strategic game, but understood she had to wrap it with charm and a kind smile. The Southern twang was the bow on top. Tina understood there was a "soccer mom" archetype she was there to fill, and she played to it without letting that prevent her deft strategic navigation of the game. As viewers were still warming to the ideas of strategy and manipulation, Tina waded into the water with them, carefully, rather than throwing them into the deep end. And in doing so, she may have saved the show.

EVERY HERO NEEDS their villain. And—especially in the early aughts—when your hero is the rugged all-American mama's boy, what better foil than the mouthy LA flirt?

As aspiring actress **Jerri Manthey** massaged Colby's back in the third episode of her first season, her legacy was already being written. She wasn't the tribe's weakest player or the most scheming. She wasn't especially mean. But she was a woman with strong opinions, irritating habits, and she flirted, hard, with the tribe's golden boy. She was perfect for the role the show needed her to play: *Survivor*'s first villainess.

Jerri gave production plenty to work with. She was stubborn. She argued with Keith (the chef) over how to cook rice. Even the never-negative Tina says, "Oh, Jerri—love her heart, I love her now, she is just a different human being now. But out there, she was just quite difficult, she was a very difficult person." Perhaps most importantly, Jerri played the seductress, trying to lure hero Colby.

At first, Colby leaned into the flirtation, saying he enjoyed seeing how far they'd go. But the tides turned. Keith warned him, "She ain't good enough for you. I'd beat you like a dog if you two hooked up." When "Maneater Manthey," as she has been called, moaned about missing chocolate, Colby said, "She's using her thoughts of chocolate to substitute for her thoughts of sex." Adding the iconic line: "I may be a lot of things but I ain't no Hershey bar." The flirting stopped and negging began. During one challenge, Colby suggested

Jerri tie a rope around her neck. After a loss, he dumped a bucket of water on her. He lied about being aligned with her but, for the all-American hero, the lie was justified: "I didn't like the fact that I had to lie, but because I was lying to Jerri, I didn't lose sleep over it." Jerri was the hero's distraction.

Still, Jerri kept her head in the game. She stuck with her tribe, Ogakor, through the merge and cast a pivotal vote that kept Colby and Tina in power. She didn't backstab. She didn't betray. She flirted. She griped. The country had just vilified another "evil seductress" in the White House—Monica Lewinsky. And in Jerri, production found another flirty brunette. Her "villainess" edit may have been outsized, but in playing that role, she helped define an important new archetype for the show—the flirty female villain, the seductress, the Black Widow. It is a character that countless future players would return to, reinterpret, and eventually perfect.

After the earliest players established the tone and form of the game, just two seasons in it was already clear *Survivor* wasn't just a game, but a story. Production had the power to shape who could be seen as a villain and who was hailed as a hero. Manipulative gays and corrupting vixens: villains. The stalwart cowboys: heroes. But those clean-lined distinctions that seemed so easy for production at the time would quickly blur, as new players brought new stories with them and audiences learned to embrace the moral nuances of the game.

CHAPTER 2

Bigger Fish to Fry

From Players to Legends

Ethan Zohn, Vecepia Towery & Brian Heidik

AFTER RICHARD HATCH OUTWITTED HIS WAY TO $1 MILLION and Tina Wesson secured her win through subtle strategy and strong relationships, *Survivor* had now proven itself as a game with elements beyond just survival—a game of schemes, relationships, and evolving ethics. Next, it had to show that it could endure. The next era of winners—playing vastly different games from one another—proved that, despite following the same general format, the *story* of *Survivor* could be different every single season. It wasn't the challenges or locations or twists, but rather the players who made it shine. They expanded the show's ideas of how to play—and how to win.

In Seasons 3 to 5, *Survivor* juries crowned three wildly different winners: Ethan Zohn, Vecepia Towery, and Brian Heidik. Each brought a distinct approach to the game. There was a humanitarian who proved good guys could win; a lone wolf who defied the odds; and a cold strategist who treated the game like a transaction. Together, they showed there was not a single blueprint of how to win this game—but countless paths to becoming the Sole Survivor.

Ethan Zohn was the golden boy of the vaguely named *Survivor: Africa*, which was filmed in Kenya's Shaba National Reserve in the summer of 2001. He played a game that relied on social skills and was seemingly universally beloved. "He's great! What can you say [that's] negative about Ethan? Nothing!" said an exasperated Teresa "T-Bird" Cooper, a member of the opposing alliance, while trying to convince others to vote him out—a warning they never heeded. If Tina Wesson showed you can win *Survivor* while remaining kind,

Ethan proved the value of social strategy as a powerful path to victory. He was soft-spoken and emotionally open, and—perhaps thanks to his curly locks and disarming smile (a damn cutie)—found himself as social center of his season. He wasn't the one to create game-changing strategies or orchestrate blindsides, but he showed how being really, genuinely likable was a strategy of its own. He was loyal to his alliance, but good to his competitors. When Jeff asked him one of the core questions of this game—how a player can expect the jury they eliminated to vote for them to win—he focused not on gameplay, but treatment: "Well, you just gotta hope that what you did before the vote and how you treated people before the vote will put you in a good light." His jury agreed. They awarded that mentality, awarded goodwill.

Ethan's do-good attitude wasn't just a front he put on during *Survivor* to win over the jury. It seems true to who he is. Ethan had been a professional soccer player in Zimbabwe before the show, where he saw firsthand the devastation caused by the HIV/AIDS epidemic. He used his winnings to cofound Grassroots Soccer, an adolescent health organization that has made a significant global impact.[6] In his personal life, he battled cancer twice since his first *Survivor* appearance, but still returned for the fortieth season, *Winners at War*, where he won a new generation of hearts through his resilience.

A WINNER WHO has long been overlooked in *Survivor*'s lore, **Vecepia Towery** broke barriers, not only in terms of how to win the game, but *who* could win the game. In 2002, she was the first Black contestant to win *Survivor*—and, with that, the first Black winner of any US reality competition show. Vecepia played a quiet, under-the-radar game in Season 4. She's deeply religious and has said she initially hoped to play

6. Grassroots Soccer has reached 25 million young people across over sixty countries, supporting mental health programs as well as providing mentorship and helping to decrease both unwanted pregnancies and the spread of HIV.

a game "The Father" would approve of, but quickly had her "come to Jesus" moment and decided to let herself leave it all out on the island (Marquesas, in this case). Vecepia had her funny confessionals and quirky moments, but played on a tribe with some of the game's biggest characters— Rob Mariano (page 43) and Sean Rector (page 45). She was under-featured from the start, never the biggest personality. She also made sure she was never the biggest threat. She played a savvy, mostly solo game. She played from the bottom and never fully embedded herself with a group (save for the strong friendship she formed with Sean). She was the first winner to not come from a majority alliance that dominated the game. Vecepia was nimble, a lone wolf who was there to advance herself further in the main game and not participate in the sideshow antics; her tagline became "there's too much drama!" Vecepia later cited Sandra Diaz-Twine (page 61) as one of her favorite *Survivors*, but in many ways, you can see how her game might have laid a foundation for the iconic strategy for which Sandra became known. Vecepia's jury rewarded her ability to outlast.

SURVIVOR'S FIFTH SEASON, set in Thailand and airing in fall 2002, is one of the least popular in the show's history. There's a general offensiveness and negativity that looms, and much of that might stem from the player who dominated the season, **Brian Heidik**. The used car salesman became known for approaching *Survivor* as a "business trip." It was all a negotiation; he kept things cool, calculated, and emotionally distant. He made alliances with many, but kept few. Despite his aloof affect, alliance hopping, and boatload of sexist jokes, Brian's tribemates still seemed to trust and even like him—until he turned on them. Ever the salesman, he knew to act like a strong ally and friend in front of his fellow players, while telling the camera he didn't care about anyone but himself. Brian's most lasting contribution to *Survivor*, however, is his inauguration of the "goat strategy"—stringing along a weak or disliked player you think you can beat at the end. In his season he brought Clay Jordan, who was equally unpopular but also seen as feckless. While Brian's backstabbing and manipulation meant he eventually faced the ire of an angry jury in the finale, he still won in a 4–3 vote. He proved that, with a bad enough competitor, you can still win the game. Even a jury full of people you screwed over would reward "the lesser of two evils," as former tribemate Ted Rogers called him.[7]

Just two seasons later, Brian's ruthless victory was a far cry from the heart-based win of Ethan. *Survivor* was officially a game of infinite possibilities, and the next era of players would complicate that, bringing their own stories and own identities to the show each season.

7. The "goat strategy" is one many have adopted since, and is likely a contributing factor to production eventually switching to a three-person finale starting in Season 13.

Rob Mariano
& Sean Rector

BOSTON ROB IS PROBABLY THE MOST RECOGNIZABLE NAME IN the *Survivor* world. He has become a face of the show, and would undoubtedly be on anyone's *Survivor* Mt. Rushmore (an apt comparison, given both entities' unideal imprints on tribal cultures). The other faces on this hypothetical reality show monument might be debated—Richard Hatch (page 11), Sandra Diaz-Twine (page 61), Cirie Fields (page 105), Parvati Shallow (page 89), and Tony Vlachos (page 174) are all strong contenders—but every list would include Boston Rob.

Rob Mariano was a construction worker from Canton, Massachusetts (a historic town just south of Boston) and part of an Italian American family. He first appeared on Season 4, *Survivor: Marquesas*, in 2002, with Vecepia. He was twenty-six years old and spoke with a thick Boston accent. He wore a black tank top, a gold chain around his neck, and a sometimes-backward New England sports cap (in his first season, it was the Patriots, but his image is most associated with a Red Sox cap). He played *Survivor* like a "mob boss." Through Rob, audiences warmed to the drama of strategy. In an era where Matt Damon and Ben Affleck brought Boston-ness to the mainstream and *The Sopranos* was peak TV, Rob was perfectly situated: *Survivor*'s first anti-hero.

Coined "The Robfather" by Jeff Probst, Mariano brought a mafioso-ish sense of theatrics to his cutthroat gameplay, molding it into something audiences wanted to root for. He remains one of reality TV's greatest masters of social manipulation: He has played *Survivor* for 152 days across five seasons, the most in the show's history, and has gone on to master the genre, appearing on *The Amazing Race* twice, *Deal or No Deal Island*, *The Traitors*, and more.

One of the defining moments that established Rob in the lore of *Survivor* came early in his first season. Rob's Maraamu tribe was terrible, the worst the show had seen yet—they lost every single challenge in the first several episodes. Despite continuously facing eliminations at Tribal Council, there was one player whose name was seemingly never on the chopping block: Hunter Ellis. Hunter was this season's Colby. He was sharp-nosed and blonde, a former fighter pilot. He looked like Val Kilmer in *Top Gun*. He was the tribe's leader, the biggest muscle, and, arguably, the hardest worker (or at least most vocal about being a hard worker). He was popular with his tribemates, production and later the audience. In this early era of the show, when tribe strength and survival skills were still top priorities, players like Hunter were largely untouchable, at least until the merge.

But Rob had different plans for the tribe. He wanted to be the alpha—and he would win that standing through cunning rather than brawn. Rob wanted control. And Ellis posed as his biggest threat.

Leaning against a tree, shirtless, wearing his gold chain and a smug smile, Rob spoke slowly in his swaggering Boston drawl and gave a confessional monologue that would come to define his legendary gameplay:

It's important to me to have people on my team who are going to do what I tell them to do and not know that I'm telling them to do it. It doesn't matter if my team is stronger physically or even stronger mentally, but just that they obey. . . . Fear basically. It's a tough principle, but fear keeps people loyal. If they're afraid they have something to lose, then they'll do what [you] tell them to do. That's straight out of The Godfather. *It's true.*

As he made this iconic speech, the cameras cut to shots of him checking in with the other members of his tribe, shaking hands and patting backs. The Robfather was assuming control.

That night at Tribal Council, Ellis was eliminated in a shocking blindside. It was fantastic TV—a moment that made a master.

"I MEAN, THAT'S not exactly how it went down," **Sean Rector** tells me. Sean was there on Marquesas, on the same doomed tribe with Rob. The two of them were tight allies and are still good friends. Sean says *he* approached Rob with the idea of eliminating Ellis. "I was like, 'We gotta get this motherfucker out now.'"

They strategized together, but Sean understood he had to let Rob lead. "When you're Black, you gotta lead from the back," he says. "As long as the goal is met, I don't care."

There's not even a hint of this on the show itself: No hushed conversations between the coconspirators or insightful confessionals from Sean framing his choice to let those around him take the visible lead. We didn't hear this perspective. Instead, viewers got a fantastic monologue from Rob. It was valuable to his story, building out his lore and establishing him as a *force majeure*. But that was just one perspective. Despite outlasting Rob by fifteen days, Sean was given a different edit by the producers: the comic relief.

"I feel like they didn't give me credit at all, throughout," Sean says of his edit. "I just happened to be there, saying cute, funny stuff from time to time."

Sean is funny—several of his on-screen moments made me laugh out loud—but he is also more than that. He was a bright and unique player. No one can be fully represented in an edit of a reality show, but certain players get the privilege of a far more multi-dimensional edit than others. In a show that reaches audience screens, showcasing "real life" but filtered through the perspectives of its producers, who gets to become the star? Which stories get to be told?

———

SEAN RECTOR GREW up in New York City, in Harlem. He was raised by a single mother, with help from the Dominican "abuela" who lived next door. Growing up in Harlem in the 1970s and 1980s, a vibrant and culturally rich community with deep Black history, Sean had a keen sense of identity. His grandmother was a Civil Rights activist who had worked to integrate schools. He grew up alongside hip hop. "I just come from that lineage," he says. He dealt with prejudiced teachers and racist police officers. He had friends and classmates from all over the world. "We had Russian neighbors and Jewish neighbors and Latinos. I was almost bilingual," he says. "New York kids, we just had this chutzpah."

Then Rector brought this chutzpah to rural Pennsylvania. For high school, Sean was accepted to the prestigious Milton Hershey boarding school, with free admission. His family was thrilled, but Sean wasn't so sure. "I'm finding myself, hip hop, girls. And I'm ready for the ninth grade. It's New York, it's the '80s. It's everything you see in the movies. And then I go get accepted and it's cows, it's farming, it's a whole lot of white people, it's a lot of structure."

This dichotomy created some friction for Sean early on. He was an "unpolished inner city kid" in a formal, institutional space. "Because I know my history, I would enter these predominantly white spaces with a sort of bravado, and they was like, 'Who's this little mother-fucker? Who are you?' " This meant trouble early for Sean, but eventually he found his rhythm. He learned, in the way many minorities in traditional (read: white) spaces must, how to speak multiple cultural languages—how to lean just enough to meet the expectations society places on you while not tipping over, while still remaining yourself. Sean's experience at Milton Hershey taught him that he could find common ground and integrate with all sorts of people, a valuable skill on *Survivor*, but he never lost that Harlem chutzpah.

Sean graduated from Milton Hershey and went to college at SUNY Albany, studying theater. After successful acting stints in New York, including on Broadway, he went to Los Angeles for pilot season auditions, supplementing his income with substitute teaching. He submitted an audition video for *Survivor* but didn't think much of it. He was regularly submitting auditions to all sorts of things; "it could have been for *The Dating Game 2* for all I knew." But Rector distinctly remembers a Black student telling him: "You should go on *Survivor,* being that you always teach us how our people survive."

It was Rector's quintessential "bravado," a wry playfulness with the construct of authority, that helped him excel in his *Survivor* interviews. "There were always people in high spaces that appreciated that, 'cause they were so used to people kissing their ass and I'm not stupid," he says.

When Sean was cast, he didn't realize how "real" *Survivor* would be. He showed up for filming in a long leather jacket and a cool hat, "my whole New York vibe look." As the castaways began their trip to French Polynesia on planes, boats, cars—"rickety shit"—it got hotter and hotter as they neared the equator, and he had to shed layers. During this season's frenzied opening scene, Sean watched, shocked, as everyone else jumped off the looming ship into the open ocean. He thought, "'And cut,' like, when is the cut coming so we can go to the next location?" Jeff told him he needed to jump, he'd be paddling there.

"Dude, ocean and beach is two different things. Jumping in the ocean water was crazy," Rector says. But he eventually jumped—he didn't have much of a choice—and with this oceanic initiation, had his baptism into the very real world of *Survivor.* With no craft service stations for the contestants in sight, and the hunger that quickly followed, Sean realized just how real this experience would be. He put his game face on.

Sean connected with Rob because of Rob's no-nonsense, blue-collar mentality. "I always found a way to connect with all kinds of people . . . I'm a social chameleon. Put me anywhere and I'm going to thrive. The only thing you can't change is race," Sean says. The two became coconspirators and remain friends. A few episodes after the Hunter elimination, both played an integral role in *Survivor*'s first filmed flip (given Tina Wesson's from Season 2 was unfilmed and

I want to take a moment here to emphasize just how harsh the conditions on *Survivor* are. Players are starving—in the earlier seasons, they were given minimal amounts of rice, reportedly enough for about one cup a day each. But as of *Survivor 41*, rice is no longer guaranteed, and the "rice negotiation," where players are given the chance to trade rewards for rice, has become a new hallmark. There may be a successful fishing trip, or a crab is found and picked through and shared. Some players resort to eating earth worms or ants, any morsels of protein. This is compounded with the physical fatigue from the grueling challenges (things I doubt I could do at my healthiest) and mental fatigue from the strategizing and second-guessing. There is no escape from the elements—save the shoddy shelters made out of bamboo and palm fronds—even during heat waves and lightning storms. Their bodies are torn up with bug bites. *Survivor* has had many medical evacuations—as many as three apiece in the *Kaôh Rōng* and *Micronesia* seasons—but even the players who last experienced life-changing effects on their body and mind. "Big Tom" Buchanan from *Survivor: Africa* reportedly lost eighty pounds while on the show. "America's Sweetheart" Colleen Haskel had larvae growing under her skin after the first season. Just days into *Kaôh Rōng*, contractor Jennifer Lanzetti spent the night in intense pain when a bug crawled into her ear canal. (The cameras even caught the moment when it crawled back out the next morning.) Players have returned home with all sorts of parasites and infections, plus mental scars. This book largely focuses on the social world and strategy of the game, but it is important to remember the intense material context in which these stories are taking place.

unexplained). At the merge, they knew they were down in numbers and could easily be Pagong-ed by the other (Rotu) tribe's seemingly tight, seven-person alliance. To save themselves, they identified the three players who seemed to be at the bottom, convincing them along with Vecepia to join an "outsider's alliance," flipping the numbers and the game on its head. Rob helped introduce the idea, but was eliminated. Sean executed it.

Rob and Sean both made for fantastic TV. Rob had his masterful musing monologues on social control—just three seasons after Richard Hatch was vilified for his manipulations, Rob was celebrated for this style of gameplay. Meanwhile, Sean brought energy and witty commentary to the show. He started a "morning show" on the beach, a radio spoof where he would "call in" his tribemates as correspondence on music, weather, and island life. He sang and danced. And Sean brought his chutzpah to *Survivor*, the unique perspective shaped by his upbringing, so different from that of his other castmates.

On Marquesas, players were being eaten alive by nono flies— blood sucking sand flies that left big welts on their bodies. On an episode of the "morning show," when Hunter shared an update saying black flies' bites were worse than the white ones, Sean "called in" to joke: "This is a conspiracy! Why do the black nono's have to be the worst ones on the island? The white ones are just as bad. The black ones get blamed for all the bad. They incarcerate all the black nonos, all the black nonos get in trouble with the law."

Like much of what Sean says, it was wrapped in a joke, but in reality, he was doing something radical here. Sean was the first player to speak openly about being Black on *Survivor* (at least that viewers saw) and the ways it shapes people's perceptions.

"Sometimes the game isn't necessarily fair, because me and [Vecepia] are playing a whole 'nother mental game that they don't even know, that when you're a person of color and you're the only one you have to play," Sean shared in one of his confessionals. "That's something they don't have to worry about, everybody can just be themselves. We have to be ourselves but then hold back a little bit."

By articulating this reality, Sean cracked open the myth that *Survivor* was a perfectly level playing field. He forced viewers to see that if the show is a microcosm of society, then society's hierarchies and inequities come with it—especially when production may bring their own biases to both the game and the editing room. In our conversation more than twenty years later, Sean adds: "Regardless of the game of survival, the game of life still applies. . . . In a show that's based on social gain, whites are gonna have an intrinsic advantage." The openness with which Sean carried his race ultimately became a boon to the show.

Core to *Survivor* is the idea that people from different worlds, with different perspectives, are forced to unite to survive. In what is considered an all-time great episode—and was that season's submission for the Emmy Awards—Sean went on a reward challenge with fellow castaway Paschal English. Sean was the young Black kid from Harlem, Paschal the older white judge from Georgia.

Two Marquesan men arrived with horses, ready to take them to an awaiting Polynesian feast. Sean wasn't so sure: "The only horse I've ever been on is the merry-go-round in Central Park," he said. Eventually, he rode together with one of the locals, holding on for dear life while expressing, politely, "Uh, my balls—My balls really hurt, sir." Paschal laughed and, later, over a mouthwatering feast and lively Polynesian dance performance, this unlikely pair became fast friends. By the time they headed back to camp, they weren't just allies, they were, as the episode title declared, "two peas in a pod." "Two days ago, I would have mortgaged my house on the fact that Sean was going to be voted off. But things have dramatically changed . . . I feel very close to him. I feel very fortunate to know him. That's what's good about this game, you never know what's going to happen," Paschal said.

It was entertaining. Sean is deeply funny, but it was also strategic.

Sean saved himself with his charm. It was one of those special "only on *Survivor*" moments—two seemingly opposite personalities, forging connection and friendship within these absurd circumstances—and it resonated so well because identity was looming large, thanks to Sean bringing it into the conversation and acknowledging the reality of it.

Rob was eliminated right after the merge; he didn't actually make the jury this season. Sean made it to fifth, voted out once his Outsiders Alliance was forced to turn on each other. But both were standout characters of the season—in part, due to Vecepia's low-key game and edit. After the show aired, both Rob and Sean received lots of attention from the public and the media, much of it positive, though Sean recalls hate mail with death threats and racial slurs too. Sean had several acting opportunities come up and holding deals in the works, but since he was still under contract with *Survivor*'s production company, they "nixed" them.

Four seasons later, both Sean and Rob were contacted about returning for *Survivor: All-Stars*, set to air in the spring of 2004.

Rob returned and played a dominant game, closely aligned with Amber Brkich from Season 2. (Brkich wasn't particularly memorable in *Australia*, hidden among the cat-and-mouse of Colby and Jerri, but casting director Lynne Spillman had stayed in touch with her and seen how much she had grown.) Together, Rob and Amber executed impressive blindsides and watched each other's backs—they forever elevated the threat level of a tight duo on *Survivor*. And their duo wasn't just for show—on the Panamanian beaches under an infinitely starry sky, a romance blossomed. They made it to the end together, with Rob winning the final Immunity Challenge and choosing to bring Amber to the finale. At the live reunion, just before the votes were read, Rob pulled out a ring and proposed. Amber said yes, without hesitation. Then the votes were read and she won the $1 million. Watching both their gameplay and romance build and bloom over the course of a season, ending with this swooning success, remains one of the most exciting moments in *Survivor*'s history.[8]

Sean, meanwhile, went through the casting process for *All-Stars*. He arranged childcare for his son and time-off with the principal of the school he worked at. "And then the day we were supposed to leave, I was sitting there with my girlfriend waiting," but he never got the final call. "It was embarrassing, it was hurtful," he says.

Rob would come back to play several more times, perfecting his Robfather gameplay and cementing his legacy as one of *Survivor*'s best players. He built a new archetype for a dominating, cult leader-like strategy. In future seasons, he would cultivate tight, deeply loyal alliances by making each member feel important, but also afraid of what might happen if they turned on Mariano. He would use the looming possibility of a secret hidden idol to instill fear, regardless of whether he actually had it in his possession. He famously created a "buddy system" to ensure each member of his alliance was always accounted for, and no one could sneak off and strategize a coup. Rob would finally win in 2011 on Season 22, *Redemption Island*, his fourth time playing.

Boston Rob is particularly good at *Survivor*. In the game, he is a competitive physical threat and a unique strategist. Onscreen, he is a great character, the mob boss who makes for exciting TV. He is deserving of his spot as one of the greatest of all time. He is still married to his *Survivor* sweetheart, Amber, with whom he has four daughters.

Sean's post-*Survivor* life has been important and fulfilling in a different way. He had other fish to fry. While substitute teaching between auditions, he found he loved working with kids, especially "in the hood"—and he had a knack for it. He became a teacher and a basketball coach. Now, he serves as the president and CEO of the TYME Foundation (Teaching Young Men Excellence), a non-profit

---

8. CBS squeezed all the juice they could from it, including a 2005 special, *Rob and Amber Get Married.*

he built based on the needs he saw during his time as a coach. "I'm like a surrogate father to thousands," Sean says. TYME offers enrichment programs to create structure in the lives of these young people to prevent gang influence and build confidence. Over 20,000 kids have come through the program.

After the initial sting of his *All-Stars* rejection, Sean figured he was done with *Survivor*. "I came, I saw, I conquered," he says. "God was like, 'I got something else for you. You gonna be in the hood, helping these boys and girls.' I'm like, 'really, Lord, you brought me all the way out here in the hood with this gang shit?'" Sean jokes. But in reality, he feels "deeply blessed" for the work he is able to do.

Sean has also spoken openly about his experience on the show and the changes he thought were needed. He says, unlike others who he believes are part of a "cult following" of not criticizing the show in order to get asked back, he was happy to be blunt, because "they ain't calling my Black ass anyway."[9]

Still, Sean remains one of the most requested players to return among fans in online chatter. Casting did reach out to him about *Survivor*'s fiftieth season. He was initially hesitant, but he wanted the opportunity for his kids, now twenty-one and eight, to see him play. Once again he went through the significant casting process: getting in shape, psychological testing, interviews. He even had to submit blood samples. He says when he interviewed with Jeff, his hackles were up given his past criticism of the show. He wasn't sure what type of welcome he would receive. "Jeff gets on the Zoom call and the first thing he says is, 'Sean, I want to apologize.'" Per Sean, Jeff said he and production had been wrong at times, and Sean was right to call them out. It lowered Sean's walls to fully commit to a casting process he was initially hesitant about. But, once again, Sean didn't get the final call.

9. Other players, too, have spoken about this "economy" of staying in the good graces of Jeff Probst to be positioned for future opportunities. Another tricky layer added to the game!

———

EVERY PLAYER ON *Survivor* brings with them their story, whether told explicitly or not. Sean's story is inextricably linked to race. "The construct of race, though it's not ours, is something we've always had to wear," he says. His Blackness, and how it shapes his world, is an integral part of Sean and was always going to be a part of the story he told. In 2004, for *All-Stars,* his wasn't a story *Survivor* (or the corporate entities shaping it) ultimately prioritized telling. Twenty years later, it seemed like that story might finally be included in *Survivor 50.* It was one many hoped for. But, again, it wasn't a story the show decided to tell.

Rob's story—that incredible saga of finding love and having children, his shaping of strategy and this entire reality genre through his booming, captivating personality—is told beautifully through *Survivor.* His life is linked to the show. Sean didn't necessarily want that life. Sure, the financial benefits of it would have been nice, and he laments some of the acting opportunities he couldn't pursue, but he feels blessed for the life he has and—though he rejects the praise—the real impact he has been able to make. Sean's *Survivor* story was cut short; his edit was limited, abbreviated. And the ways he might have shaped the show, and the conversations that came from it, remain a mystery.

After playing closely together back in the early days, Sean and Rob's *Survivor* experiences took them in very different directions. One became an icon of the show, while one never returned. We got Boston Rob, but imagine if we had also gotten Harlem Sean—a character who would have undoubtedly brought chutzpah and spunk, laugh-out-loud moments and strategic gameplay, song and dance, and importantly, representation.

Rupert Boneham

AFTER COLBY DONALDSON'S DOMINATING POPULARITY (PAGE 29), the production team seemed eager to find their next fan favorite. They thought they knew what that looked like, casting carbon copies of Colby season after season: men with washboard abs, chiseled jawlines and kind smiles; but none quite hit the same. Then came **Rupert Boneham.**

Big, burly, and dressed in a now-iconic tie-dye tank with a scraggly beard and long, brown hair, Rupert was a far cry from Colby's Ken-doll look. The "Troubled Teen Mentor" seemed like the type of guy who says "arrrgh" a lot—and he was a dream pick for *Survivor*'s pirate-themed seventh season, airing in 2003. Set in the Pearl Islands, this season was a nod to the piratical history off of Panama's coast, and Rupert was thrilled to play the part.

With the novelty of *Survivor* alone wearing off, production turned to twists and themes. This season began with a *Survivor* first: The contestants were on a boat, dressed for what they thought were publicity photos—in dresses, nice suits, and high-heeled shoes. Then they were abruptly told the game was starting. They had to swim to a tiny fishing village nearby to barter for whatever supplies they needed. Exhausted from the swim in his thick denim—"why did I wear my fancy jeans?"—Rupert was resting at his raft when the opposing Morgan Tribe left theirs, filled with shoes they had taken off for their swim, next to him. "This is definitely a pirate adventure. Pirates pillage, pirates steal, pirates take advantage," he said. He stole the shoes from the Morgan raft and bartered them for supplies for his team. "Arrrgh, it's a hard life, the pirate life," he can be heard saying as jaunty shanty music plays and the episode cuts to commercial. It's an opening scene for this themed season that couldn't have been better if scripted.

Rupert innately understood how to make good TV. This didn't just mean leaning into the theme; it meant playing the game with wit and originality and being unapologetically profuse. When his jeans were chafing, he made a skirt out of the bottoms of two of his tribemates dresses which he wore the rest of the season. When he found an injured snake, he kept it as a pet and named it Balboa. When he saw a fish he didn't recognize—a saltwater catfish—he excitedly exclaimed, "I didn't know they made such an animal!"

Boneham was charming and funny; he was deeply loyal; he seemed "good."[10] He understood he was on TV, but kept his performance rooted in authenticity, in real vulnerability. He presented himself as the redeemed underdog. When another contestant mocked his makeshift skirt and his "plumber's crack," Rupert confronted him, saying, "You took the role that every jock has taken in my life." He later added in his confessional: "I portray a strong and independent person, but in my head, I'm that fat little terrified kid who was picked on in school all his life." Rupert's vulnerability made him relatable to many viewers. He was an underdog they could enjoy rooting for. And completing the redemption arc, he often outperformed the "jocks" in challenges. As a successful spear fisherman, became the best provider for his tribe in the game. He was, in the end, too likable, and was eliminated because the other players deemed him too big of a threat to win the game.

Rupert expanded the definition of what a fan-favorite player could look like. He didn't have to be the chiseled, all-American; he could play himself: loyal to a fault, vulnerable, funny, and larger-than-life.

10. Rupert's big heart was evident on-screen and held up outside the show as well. Boneham has devoted his life to his charity, Rupert's Kids, which helps at-risk youth in his home state of Indiana.

He wasn't that Captain America figure one might idealize, but the blue-collar everyman to whom people could relate.[11]

After *Pearl Islands,* Rupert returned the very next season for *All-Stars*—becoming the first player to compete in back-to-back seasons. Though he again didn't win the game, he won a $1 million prize in "America's Tribal Council," a fan favorite vote, in which he beat players like Colby Donaldson and Boston Rob. He returned again as a "hero" in *Survivor*'s legendary twentieth season, *Heroes vs. Villains* in 2010, and then again in Season 27, *Blood vs. Water,* in 2013, where he returned with his wife Laura. After Laura was voted out by her tribe just moments into the game, he fulfilled his heroic archetype and chose to take her place so that she could continue playing, saying, "I love *Survivor,* but I love my wife more." Though he was the first player out, Rupert had already solidified his legacy and highlighted the importance of unique, fun, and vulnerable characters on *Survivor.*

11. He even tried to bring this populist energy to the Indiana Gubernatorial Race in 2012, running as a Libertarian, but ended up losing to Mike Pence with just 3.9 percent of the votes.

Jonny Fairplay

PEARL ISLANDS BROUGHT VIEWERS ONE OF THE SHOW'S MOST
beloved players in Rupert, but also one of the show's most despicable villains: **Jonny Fairplay**. Fairplay was the perfect antagonist to Rupert—conniving and disloyal, lanky with a punchable face and mop of curly bleach blonde hair. He would call names and pick fights, drink himself silly with the jugs of booze he had bartered for, and make lewd jokes about naked teenage girls. As Rupert put it: "Jon, he reminds me of my boys who I mentor who just pop off *stupid* stuff. You know, talk about gettin' some honey or smokin' sum'n, drinkin' sum'n." Ultimately, Fairplay orchestrated Rupert's blindside.

Ruthlessly booting the fan favorite was just the beginning of Fairplay's villainy. One of the most coveted rewards on *Survivor* were the family visits. Reunited across thousands of miles, parents and partners run down the beach into their loved ones' arms. Always an emotional visit after a long, hard month, these rewards provided a much needed emotional boost to players. But they were only allowed a short hug with their loved ones—they had to win the challenge to get to spend more time together. This season, Fairplay's friend, Dan, arrived on the beach, running up to Fairplay with a big smile. They gave each other a tight hug before Fairplay asked, "Oh dude, how's Grandma?" Dan's smile dropped. "She died, dude." Fairplay looked down, heartbroken. He told his tribe, with an emotional tremble in his voice, "It was either going to be my buddy or my grandmother coming, and my grandmother's not here for a reason."

The other players decided to let Fairplay win the challenge, giving up their special opportunity to spend this time with their families so that Fairplay could learn more from Dan and grieve his grandma. They held his hand and gave him long, caring hugs. The losing players didn't even get to say goodbye to their loved ones. Instead, they were forced to go to an entirely new island with no food or shelter, while Fairplay and Dan stayed together at camp. One of the contestants, scoutmaster Lillian Morris, explained: "I wish I could see [my husband] and just talk to him for a few more minutes, but then Jon got his news about his grandmother. . . . My husband has to understand that this is what we had to do." They arrived at their barren island, hoping they could make a fire with a long, exposed night ahead of them.

Cut to: Fairplay back at camp, laughing with Dan. "That was a brilliant performance, sir," he said, giving his friend a high five. "My grandmother's sitting at home watching *Jerry Springer* right now," he told the cameras as they enjoyed a night together at camp. His grandmother was very much alive.

There are levels to the lies told on *Survivor*. Until this moment, lies were mechanics of gameplay—false promises about an alliance or throwing someone's scent off of an upcoming boot. Fairplay threw that unspoken rule out of the window, opening the door for emotional manipulation and lying about "real life" in a game that was previously mostly self-contained.

Fairplay's cheekiness revealed something unique about his understanding of this game. He knew the cameras were watching, and in this game, he was a player, both in the strategic and theatrical sense. If Rupert "performed" by leaning into his authentic self, by sharing his vulnerabilities openly, Jonny Fairplay, in fact, was just a character.

His real name is Jon Dalton. Jon came to *Survivor* from the world of professional wrestling, where he played a "heel"—the figure in wrestling meant to be booed and jeered, rooted against. The heel plays as the antagonist to the hero. They play by their own rules; they're intentionally offensive, they cheat and scheme. It might not be the most upstanding role, but it's essential to the storytelling, keeping the audience entertained and emotionally invested. With his experience from the wrestling world, Fairplay understood that you can play this game as a character, and he chose to be the *Survivor* heel.

Players like Richard Hatch and Jerri Manthey were made the villain. Fairplay anticipated it, got ahead of it. He put himself in the role and gave production all the material they could wish for. This kind of understanding of performance would become commonplace in *Survivor*, but Fairplay was one of the first to explicitly perform a type. While Jon Dalton may not lie about his grandmother, for Jonny Fairplay, it was fair game.

Sandra Diaz-Twine

SANDRA DIAZ-TWINE HAD BIG PLANS FOR HER *SURVIVOR* AUDITION video. She had discussed it with her neighbors who lived in the same apartment building at the Fort Lewis Army Base—all *Survivor* fans. She imagined coming out in her uniform and barking orders at them like a drill sergeant, scolding the lazy ones sleeping under a tree.

Sandra Diaz-Twine watched *Survivor* regularly, but hadn't thought about applying until she heard Jeff Probst encourage it at a finale: "If you think you have what it takes to win, go to CBS.com and apply."

"I play the lottery, I play bingo. Where else do you have the chance to go out and have a one in sixteen chance at a million dollars?" Sandra thought. She and her husband had gifted themselves a computer and printer for Christmas, so she went online and printed out the application. "It was over a hundred pages," she says.

She carefully filled out the written application. *Which player are you most like?* "Boston Rob." *What are the top three reasons you want to play Survivor?* "The money. The money. The money." It took her months to do the written portion. Then, it was time to film that video she had planned, and "no one would help me," she says. "So now I'm in my kitchen pissed off." Even her husband had reservations, telling her: "You only hear what you want to hear, you love to gossip, you're going to be the first one voted out.'"

With everyone discounting her, Sandra picked up the camcorder, set it up onto her kitchen counter, and hit record as she looked straight into the lens:

It's me Sandra. Anyways, as you can see, I'm doing this all by myself. Why? I didn't have a choice; nobody wants to help me. But that's okay, that's cool, I don't need them nohow. You know what I'm saying? I could do this on my own . . . I can survive out there. If I can survive the heat of Miami, the heat of Puerto Rico, the heat in Louisiana . . . I spent five months in Saudi Arabia out there in the desert, I can survive anywhere you put me, it's all good, you know what I'm saying? It don't matter to me. I gotta get up out of here. It's simple, I need to come back with that million dollars. Why? Because I got a hoopty for a ride and I live in a damn rat hole and that ain't no damn lie . . . I'm pleading, I am begging, bring me out to Survivor, remember this face, save me a place on Survivor, 'cause I really need it, and you won't regret it.

Production did bring Sandra out to *Survivor*. And they certainly didn't regret it. She became the first two-time winner in *Survivor* history, her legacy signaling the start of the show's evolving lore that would transform it from weeknight entertainment to a living mythology.

SANDRA WAS RAISED by her single mother and her maternal grandparents, bouncing between Puerto Rico, Miami, and Connecticut. She quickly learned how to adapt, making new friends as she moved around, integrating herself into cities with very different cultures and social scenes. That flexibility was visible in her *Survivor* game: "You gotta roll with the punches," she says.

At seventeen, Sandra enlisted in the army with the plan of getting the GI Bill to fund her college education. It was there that she met her husband, Marcus. They had two daughters together. Still, Sandra stuck to the plan. "We say what we are gonna do and we always stick to it," she says.

Diaz-Twine went to school, getting a degree in Business Administration while also working and taking care of her daughters, even when Marcus was deployed. She remembers doing homework at

McDonald's so her daughters could run around the colorful tubes and slides of the PlayPlace while she studied. A schedule like this is unequivocally difficult, but Sandra is matter of fact about this phase of her life: "I just always made it happen," she says now. "When you want to make it work, and you know the reasons why, you make it work."

One April 1st, 2003, Sandra and family had just moved to a different house on the base. Right after she set up her landline, the phone rang—the very first call she got was from *Survivor*, requesting she come to Seattle for an interview the next day. It wasn't an April Fool's prank. "I was like, 'No, I gotta get my hair and my nails done.' But I don't know why, because that's not even how I am." When she arrived (sans manicure), she greeted other applicants with "hello" and "good morning." No one responded. "I remember saying, 'well, fuck you too.' Those were my exact words." Only later did she see the sign on the wall: PLEASE DO NOT SPEAK TO EACH OTHER.

Sandra impressed in her interviews with her sassy spark and tell-it-how-it-is mentality. She also brought something else important to the screen: representation.

Just three months before *Survivor* began filming her season, the United States invaded Iraq. Sandra was military, a soldier's wife in the early aughts. She was a working mom, juggling school and kids. Competing on the show's seventh season, Sandra was also only the second player of Latin American origin to play *Survivor*. She remembers Jeff Probst telling her, "Oh, you're just gonna be another Jessie Camacho. You guys are all talk." (Camacho, also Puerto Rican, was voted off *Survivor: Africa* in Episode 2 after getting sick from drinking contaminated spring water.) Sandra responded: "No, put my ass out there and I'm going to show you that I will do whatever it takes."

Sandra represented working mothers, military families, Latinas—a departure from the mostly white, athletic, young people who made up the bulk of the casts at the time—and with this she would bring a new mentality to the game, a new kind of work ethic.

Sandra *made it work*. In that opening barter scene, while Rupert Boneham (page 55) stole the show with his dazzling shoe theft, it was Sandra who set her team up for success. While other contestants begged, pushed, and argued, Sandra stayed cool and collected. She spoke to the locals in fluent Spanish, negotiating with respect and a no-nonsense tone that would become a quintessential feature of her gameplay. She was there to "get shit done." While the members of the opposing team ran around the market yelling in broken English, Sandra joked comfortably with local vendors. She was even invited to a backyard barbecue, where she traded her gold chain for everything there, taking sizzling chicken legs straight off the grill. "We didn't take that grill because it didn't have wheels or we would've took it too, like for real," she says.

Sandra was, admittedly, never a physical competitor. In group challenges, she became known as the sit-out queen. In her four seasons playing *Survivor*, she never won a single individual immunity. In fact, several of her original *Pearl Islands* tribemates have said that if they'd lost the first challenge—one they won by mere feet—this icon of the franchise would've likely been the first one out. But Sandra found a way to slip through, and make it work.

It is this keen understanding of how others perceive her that is the key to Sandra's game. Like her husband and neighbors before, her tribemates underestimated her. In the second episode, Jonny Fairplay assured producers Sandra was no threat in a confessional: "We have bigger fish to fry first. But she's not one of the final four. And I got a million that says she won't be the final one," he said. Little did he know.

Sandra knew she was being overlooked. So, she *made it work* for herself, using her social savvy to fly under the radar and pin targets to other players' backs.[12] She says she pushed the idea that "there's

---

12. When Rupert Boneham—who had become her closest *Pearl Islands* ally— was blindsided, Sandra set out to get revenge in one of the most deliciously petty moments of the game. She remembers Jonny Fairplay telling her and fellow ally

always bigger fish to fry, you can get to me later." Later turned out to be too late.

As the strategy on *Survivor* became increasingly convoluted, Sandra remembers watching from her couch and thinking some players were overthinking things. "As long as it ain't you, who gives a damn who goes home," she says. This mentality underlined Sandra's now famous "anyone but me" strategy. While others schemed to control the board, Sandra let the chaos swirl around her—often sparking it herself—without ever getting swept up, a mode of play rooted less in domination than in endurance. In the social microcosm of *Survivor*, invisibility could be its own kind of power.

Sandra deftly guided conversations without directly telling anyone what to say or think, redirecting blame and turning up the heat on arguments to make other players "look like [they're] the bad guy so that [they're] the next one picked on," she says.

At the final three, scoutmaster Lillian Morris picked Diaz-Twine to come to the finale, preferring the fellow mother to the villainous Fairplay. As Sandra made her case to the jury, she proved she understood her game the whole time: "Other people had other agendas, other fish to fry . . . I was willing to give up whoever, as long as it wasn't me." She added, "Maybe because I'm Puerto Rican, I know that if I don't look out for number one, nobody else gonna look out for me."

Sandra left the island happy. She didn't think she would win the million, but she knew she at least had $100,000, the prize guaranteed to second place. She immediately went back to work, where she was welcomed with open arms and slight concern about her dramatic weight loss after just a couple months at "another job." Since she

---

Christa Hastie, "You bitches are next." When she got back to camp, furious, she stormed over to the pot of fish Rupert had caught before his elimination, and tipped the fish bucket onto the sandy floor, where, overnight, they rotted, attracting rats. She wasn't caught in the act and, when suspicion fell on a confused Christa, Sandra stayed quiet, letting her take the blame and ire of her tribemates.

expected the hundred grand, she bought a TV and rolled it into her garage, where she hosted watch parties for the other families on the base. With friends of friends eager to watch with a contestant from the show, her parties kept getting bigger and bigger. "But I'm like, 'you gotta bring a plate, 'cause I'm not gonna feed all these people,'" she jokes.

When Sandra returned for the reunion almost a year after filming, the jury vote revealed she won the game in a sweeping 6–1 victory.

Not much changed about Sandra's life after her win. She bought that new car—something she had never had—and wrote some checks to her mom and grandparents. But Sandra stayed humble: "My family members are always bothering me, like, 'girl, you always running around with them $20 purses. Splurge, treat yourself!' And I'm like, 'yeah, but you know, it's a $20 purse, but it might have a couple of hundred dollars in it, where you have a $500 or $600 dollar purse and you got maybe $20 to your name.'"

Thirteen seasons later, Sandra returned to play on *Survivor*'s twentieth season, *Heroes vs. Villains*, where she was placed on the Villains tribe (along with Jerri Manthey, Boston Rob, and more).[13] When Jeff asked who was on the wrong tribe, "I raised my hand," she says. "Everyone's like, you're too nice." But Sandra ultimately felt she was in the right place with "funny, sarcastic people." In the opening moments of the season, riding a chopper and looking out with a cold look of determination on her face, she said: "Last time I was mean and this time I'm meaner. You know, I'll lie, I don't care. But I'll make up a good lie."

By *Heroes vs. Villains*, the game was no longer just a social experiment. *Survivor* was a saga, and Sandra was a character, stepping back into its mythology. In a season filled with iconic players and big personalities, Diaz-Twine was again underestimated—and she again

---

13. Richard Hatch was originally supposed to be part of the Villains tribe, but his legal troubles prevented him from participating.

played to this advantage. After her alliance was targeted and eliminated early, Sandra was on the chopping block before the tribes even merged. But she had to *make it work*, she knew to play to the ego of her competitors. "I said the right words," she says.

The ruthless Russell Hantz (page 97) clearly thought he was controlling the game. "I know you're the boss," she remembers telling him—even though, to cameras, she openly shared that she "can't stand [him] and can't wait for [him] to go home." She told Russell: "Just get me to the merge," so she could make the jury and give him a vote in the finale. To save herself, she even voted with the group to take out her closest friend, Courtney Yates, about whom she had said: "Me without Courtney, that's like rice without beans."

Sandra did what she had to, and she made it to the merge where (perhaps tellingly) the villains took control and picked off the remaining heroes with some stellar strategic moves (see Parvati Shallow, page 89), including an idol play by Sandra. She wasn't the flashiest player, but she was there, assessing the mood and building relationships with the players she was sending to the jury. Sandra endured.

The *Heroes vs. Villains* final four came down to Sandra, Jerri Manthey, Russell Hantz, and Parvati Shallow. Russell won the final immunity and Sandra, again, knew to say the right words. "Take me to the end. You know I can't win again; you can beat me. I'll take the $100,000," she remembers saying. Hantz was convinced of his victory, confidently telling the cameras: "I'm going to use Sandra for me to win a million dollars. She can't beat me!" Sandra did say that she would make up a good lie.

In the end, Sandra won again, in a 6-3-0 vote, beating Parvati and trouncing the player who thought she was his goat; Russell received no votes. Sandra became the Queen of *Survivor*, but her win also crowned something larger than herself—it solidified the show's own lore.

———

IT IS HARD to win a season of *Survivor*. Many have tried, unsuccessfully. It is almost impossible to win two—and Sandra Diaz-Twine was the first to do so (and, as she reminds me, the only one to do it without an all-winners season, where a two-time winner would be inevitable).[14] She understood how to get it done.

Sandra's self-awareness—her clear understanding of who she was and how she might be received—is what made her the most successful *Survivor* player ever. She wasn't the flashiest strategist, the one to most outwit. She certainly was never the most physical, the one to outplay. But she proved that, importantly, she could outlast. Sandra *made it work*, and that pragmatism—paired with her sharp, authentic wit—made her something new: a player who could name her own legend as she lived it. "Queen stays Queen," as she put it, wasn't just bravado; it was prophecy.

Sandra played a role in building *Survivor*'s mythology. Between her unfiltered humor, Rupert's gruff sweetness, and Jonny Fairplay's gleeful villainy, *Pearl Islands* showed how personality itself could drive the show. The earliest players had established the format: how the game worked. The next generation refined the strategy. By the seventh season, the players made *Survivor* not just a game to play but a world to inhabit—one filled with characters, storylines, and lore.

The very next season, *Survivor: All-Stars*, made that shift explicit. For the first time, the show brought back its own characters—Richard Hatch and Rudy Boesch and Sue Hawk, Tina Wesson and Colby Donaldson and Jerri Manthey. Boston Rob returned and married Amber, and suddenly these weren't just contestants; they were mythic figures in a growing reality-TV universe. With Queen Sandra

14. At least in the American franchise. After my conversation with Sandra, Parvati Shallow (page 89) would go on to win a second game on the Australian version of the show.

at its helm, *Survivor* entered a new phase of self-awareness, treating its players as returning heroes—or villains—in a serialized epic.

Sandra is the Queen of *Survivor*, but her coronation depended on building the foundation of that mythology. She and her *Pearl Islands* castmates built the world in which royalty could exist—a universe where once-anonymous Americans could become legends and icons.

CHAPTER 3

Icons and Idols

Shifting the Lens

Yul Kwon, Cao Boi
& Ozzy Lusth

YUL KWON SEEMED PERFECT. PLAYING ON *SURVIVOR*'S THIRTEENTH season, set in the Cook Islands, he was a rare portrayal of an Asian American man in 2006 primetime TV: both brains and brawn, neither sidekick nor stereotype. **Yul Kwon** was smart, kind, funny, athletic, and strategically dominant. Before *Survivor*, he went to Stanford University and Yale Law School, where he was an editor of the *Yale Law Review*. He clerked for a federal judge, worked in the Senate and for Google. He was ripped, with impressive pecs and a six-pack, but not intimidatingly big. He seemed deeply considerate. On *Survivor,* Yul played a noble game, trying to have as much integrity as possible, while admitting there can't be real honesty in this game of manipulation. Through impressive challenge performances and game-changing strategy he led his alliance of underdogs, once down in numbers eight to four, to the final four. Sitting next to his closest allies in one of *Survivor*'s most competitive finales, he won. He was the first Asian American to win. He used his million dollars and his platform to advocate for causes that were important to him— bone marrow donation and Asian American representation. He was called one of *People Magazine's* Sexiest Men Alive, as well as one of the Hottest Bachelors by both *People* and *Extra*. Shortly after his *Survivor* appearance, he met his wife, Sophie—set up by his castmate Brad Virata who met her at a watch party. They got married in 2009 and have two happy daughters together.

The Yul we saw on *Survivor* seemed perfect. He became one of the show's icons. But that Yul is a product of hardship and hard work.

Kwon's parents immigrated to the United States from South Korea in 1971. Yul was born in Flushing, Queens; when he was six, his family moved to the San Francisco Bay area. Growing up, he says they didn't have a lot of "material wealth"—his parents came to the States with $200 in their pocket.

Yul was one of the few Asians in his East Bay community at the time. He was a "soft, overweight kid." He spoke with a lisp. He was relentlessly bullied. Yul remembers being called anti-Asian slurs and his family home being toilet-papered, with racist messages spray-painted on their lawn. Traumatizingly, he recalls young students of color being bullied in the bathrooms of his school, pinned down and peed on. To avoid this fate, Yul wouldn't go to the bathroom, and developed paruresis, or shy bladder syndrome. This condition, coupled with social anxieties and OCD, defined his life at a young age. "I couldn't do the normal things most kids could do," Yul says. "I couldn't go to ball games, parties, the mall, movies, any of that stuff because I never knew if I would be able to go to the bathroom."

Kwon grew up feeling ashamed and alone. He didn't talk about his mental health struggles with his family. He couldn't see his place in society. It's hard to not feel seen in your community, it can become harder still when you don't see yourself represented in culture. "The rare times that you did see a person of color on screen, they're usually portrayed according to a very one-dimensional stereotype," Kwon says. "So for Asian men, it was like a Kung Fu master who could kick butt but couldn't speak English, or the Chinese cook, or the geek who couldn't get a date." Yul's biggest on-screen role model was Big Bird: "He was tall and he had lots of friends and he was yellow."

Yul says the lack of cultural representation had a "pervasive influence in terms of how I saw myself and my role in the world. I just never thought of myself as someone who fit in as part of the mainstream community. I never thought that I could grow up to become a leader." He would go on to become that representation he sought, and to become a leader as well.

A turning point came for Kwon when one of his older brother's friends died by suicide. This scared Yul, who was eleven at the time. It shook him. He could imagine getting to a place where he felt that hopeless and isolated, and didn't ever want to arrive there.

Yul remembers having a conversation with his brother, who asked him an important question: "Do you think that your essence precedes your actions, or that your actions precede your essence?" Yul had always imagined it was the former—you do the things you do because of who you are—but his brother encouraged him to consider the latter: act to become who you want to be. Do things that might scare you. Kwon decided: "Why don't I just *act* confident and see what happens?"

So, Yul decided to, each day, take a small step to confront his fears. First, maybe just raising his hand in class or talking to someone new. Later, he joined the track and field team and tried out for the water polo team. He knew he wasn't the strongest swimmer, but he spent his summer practicing the "eggbeater" kick for treading water so that, combined with the benefit of his "melon head," he could get a spot on the team as a goalie. He joined a drama class and had to perform in front of his entire school. "I felt like throwing up the entire time I was backstage . . . And then something happened that I'd never experienced before in a large social setting—I had fun." Yul consistently put himself in "structured environments that would catalyze growth." This orderly approach to self-improvement is representative of how Yul works: analytical, thoughtful, and considered.

Facing his fears head-on helped Yul learn to cope with his anxieties, and soon they no longer constrained how he lived. Still, Yul continued this habit of putting himself in environments that challenged him. After getting comfortable in college, he saw a flyer that encouraged joining the Marine Corps. "So I said, 'Yeah, you know what? That actually seems like it would be really hard.'" Yul joined the Marine Corps Officer Training—one of the most intense military trainings you can do—over his last two summers of college, which whipped him into shape and gave him discipline and confidence. There, he was again told he was "too soft" and "too educated." After a mid-point platoon survey ranked him last, Yul "figured out what I needed to change . . . I just learned a lot about myself and that gave me more confidence."

Kwon was a week away from finishing his training before his senior year, but ultimately didn't complete it after his best friend, Evan, died of leukemia. Evan was diagnosed during his sophomore year at Stanford. Yul spent much of that year organizing bone marrow drives and, even as a deep introvert, talking to local media after learning how much harder it is for people of color to find transplant matches.[15]

"*SURVIVOR* WAS KIND of like the epitome of this effort" to face his fears, Yul says. He was working at Google after his government stints when a friend in the audition process recommended him to *Survivor* casting. They were looking to recruit Asians and, from his understanding, looking to fill certain stereotypes. He was meant to be the nerd—they told him to wear glasses and a suit to his interview, even though he typically wears contacts.

Yul was cast, but he wondered if he was pushing his fear-facing too far. He was shy and introverted and not eager to be on TV. He thought back to the shy bladder syndrome that he had worked so hard to manage. "What if I went on the show and there's a camera crew following me around everywhere, and I literally couldn't go to the bathroom and this deep dark secret that I've hidden from everyone I know suddenly gets exposed to a national audience. How embarrassing and terrible would that be?"

But then he thought of himself as a kid, and how valuable this representation might be. "If I was a kid and I'd seen someone who looked like me just being on television and not being defined by

---

15. Even today, almost three-quarters of African Americans and over half of Asians and Latinos don't have a perfect match in the worldwide bone marrow donor registry, according to Gift of Life.

their race, just being a normal person, wouldn't that have helped me?" He decided it would have helped, and for that reason, this was a fear worth facing.

Unbeknownst to Yul, though, his season of *Survivor* would be defined by race.

Yul noticed lots of diversity at the Santa Monica hotel when he went down for casting interviews. He was glad to see it and imagined they might have a theme like "some sort of rainbow coalition thing." It was, in fact, the opposite. *Cook Islands* is colloquially known as the "race wars" season. In a shocking decision, even for 2006 America, the starting tribes were divided by race: African Americans, Asians, Latinos, and whites ("Caucasians").

The night before they were set to begin filming, the producers gathered the contestants and told them about the controversial theme of the season. "Oh my God, I just made a horrible mistake. This is like the worst mistake I've ever made in my life. It's just a terrible idea," Yul remembers thinking. "I thought it would likely reduce us to racial stereotypes. There's so many ways this could go wrong." He considered quitting, but then figured, "At least if I am part of this show, I might have some opportunity to influence how the game plays out."

Yul felt the added weight of playing not just as a person, but as a representative. "I was very cognizant of how this might reflect on people within my community." He wanted to play hard, but a clean, honest game. He thought: "I don't want some Asian kid to get beat up the next day" for his actions. It's a tricky needle to thread—representing his hugely diverse community to millions of viewers while playing a game built on deception. This tension made this season uniquely high-pressure: every move risked confirming or defying a stereotype for so many of the contestants.

The following day, with filming about to begin, Yul again regretted his decision. The show starts on a big sailing ship, crashing through the waves of the South Pacific. But to get there, Yul and his castmates had to ride small speedboats with the windows blacked out so they couldn't see what was going on. They waited for hours for a storm to pass, these tight, blacked out boats like buoys, bobbing among the surging waves of the vast Pacific Ocean. Yul was getting increasingly seasick. And worse, he had to pee. Others were hopping off the side to use the bathroom, Yul tried but he couldn't—it was that shy bladder of his youth coming back as he had feared. He waited, puking, miserable, and embarrassed for hours. Then, they loaded onto the big ship, Jeff appeared, a bell rang, and the game had begun.

It was, as usual, a scene of chaos as everyone grabbed what supplies they could off the boat. There were chickens flying amongst the scramble, one straight over the side of the boat. Yul's tribemate, Cao Boi, told him to jump in after. "And then as soon as I hit the water, I had this moment of clarity. I'm like, 'What the fuck am I doing? How am I gonna get back on?' I remember seeing the camera's all looking at me and I'm just like, 'Oh my God, this is it. I'm gonna drown. I'm gonna die, or I'm gonna need help. And it's gonna be so embarrassing.'" As this went on in Yul's head, he managed to grab the chicken from the open ocean and hand it to Cao Boi, still on the boat, who said he would put it in a "sleeper hold." With difficulty, Yul made his way back onto the ship. When he finally climbed onto the deck, he saw Jonathan Penner of the white Rarotonga tribe holding the very chicken that was supposed to be in a chokehold in his tribemate's arms. Cao Boi had tried, but "there's no such thing as a sleeper hold on chicken."

With the race for supplies over, Kwon and his Asian Puka Puka tribe rowed their way to their new beach. Yul felt nauseous, he desperately needed to pee, and Cao Boi, his chicken-wrestling tribemate, was making the very stereotyping jokes he was there to try to dispel. ("I can't believe so many Asians, who are so little, weigh so much . . . it's all that rice." "No one suspects these little people with slanted eyes to see anything or to be strong enough to do anything.") Yul was deeply regretting his decision.

X

CAO BOI, BORN Anh-Tuan Bui, was one of the more eccentric characters in *Survivor* to date. Unlike the rest of his tribe, who were Asian Americans, **Cao Boi** was a Vietnamese refugee. He had fled Vietnam during the war when he was eleven. The tension between these different perspectives on the Asian diasporic experience—immigrant, American, refugee—was one of the more intriguing elements of this season. While Yul and most of his tribemates were hyper-aware of their roles as representatives, making an effort to not perpetuate harmful stereotypes, Cao Boi was always ready with an off-color joke or outlandish comment. "You can have a sense of humor but if it's at the expense of a particular ethnic group, I don't think that's cool," Yul said, confronting him late one night as the jokes went on.

But Yul says he learned something valuable from Cao Boi's point of view. Cao Boi wasn't going to cater to anyone. In "obviously very different words," Yul says Cao Boi argued, "Why should I bear special responsibility or manage my own behavior to fit someone else's view of what I should or shouldn't say? Why can't I just be myself?" It was a perspective that stuck with Yul.

In 2006 America, it was rare to see multiple Asian representatives on TV at all, let alone get the chance to hear a diversity of thoughts among them on how to be a representative. Even if the racial division reflected a misguided attempt by a mostly white production to provoke drama or boost ratings, one result was a range of perspectives that television at the time almost never allowed to coexist.

On the show, Cao Boi said he never felt he quite fit in with Asian Americans, "people who are like me but not like me." He felt he belonged "in a hippie community." He was often talking about mystic practices or animal symbolism. When his tribemates had headaches, he knew a method to "pull out the bad wind," violently rubbing against their brows. They would end up with a deep red line down their forehead—but the headaches were always gone.

As Yul told the cameras in an early confessional: "Cao Boi is an interesting guy. I kind of wrote him off as a freaky kook, but in between the random, kind of inane nonsense, there are actually gems, and nuggets that are actually useful."

One of the most useful things Cao Boi introduced to *Survivor* came to him late one night, in a dream.

Cook Islands was one of the earliest seasons to introduce the Hidden Immunity Idol—a talisman that would give its finder secret immunity, safety in the game. With the threat of this unknown idol looming, Cao Boi woke up one day and began to tell Yul about a dream he had. He dreamt of an old lady shaman who was handing him all sorts of credit card applications, saying over and over that he needed three. "I thought three and three. That's how you can defeat the immunity idol, you can flush it out . . . I woke up and I go, 'Whoa! Plan Voodoo.'" Cao Boi's Plan Voodoo was the first time someone had articulated, albeit confusingly, the concept of splitting the vote to flush out the idol. With a big enough numerical advantage, an alliance could split their votes between two targets (three and three, in his example). This way, if one of the targets played the idol, the alliance would still maintain control over the vote, ensuring that the other target would receive the second-most votes and have their torch snuffed.

Not long after, Cao Boi was eliminated from the game. Though vote splitting wasn't a factor in this season, it has become a major strategic element in *Survivor,* creating some of the game's most exciting eliminations—all thanks to Cao Boi and his dream of the lady shaman with credit card applications.

YUL WAS EVENTUALLY able to pee. He says his awareness of the cameras actually dissipated quickly, as did much of his anxiety. And soon, he found himself in a prime position in the game.

In just the second episode, Kwon found the Hidden Immunity Idol on Exile Island. He solved a series of clues that ended with hours of digging with his bare hands in the hot sand. This was only the third season to introduce the hidden idols, and Yul had only seen one before leaving to film. In that season, *Guatemala*, NFL player Gary Hogeboom (masquerading as a landscaper in the game) found the idol and was forced to use it at the next Tribal Council to save himself. It got him an extra few days, but was a non-factor in the course of the season. Yul knew he wanted to use his idol to "change the game." He not only did that successfully, but he changed how players used idols forever.

He first used his idol as a trust-building tool, revealing the usually secret advantage to Becky Lee, a young lawyer and his closest ally on Puka Puka. This cemented their bond that would last the whole game—and is a strategy still seen on the show today.

Yul wanted to play this game with trusted allies, working as a team, and was wary of inadvertently establishing himself as a leader. But his tribemates were increasingly drawn to him as the days on the island passed, and he found himself, reluctantly, acting as both a strategic decision-maker and a moral compass—even in decisions as small as being the tribe's official divider of food, making sure everyone got equal portions.

Kwon's leadership would soon prove essential. Mid-season, after the tribes had swapped out of their original racially divided groups, Jeff announced a dramatic twist: the opportunity to "mutiny." As Jeff counted down, the castaways were given mere seconds to decide if they wanted to stay on their current tribe or join the other. Candice Woodcock, a medical student, stepped away from the Aitu tribe, which included Yul. At the last second, she was joined by screenwriter Jonathan Penner. Both wanted to rejoin their original tribemates with whom they'd developed early alliances (the whites—an unfortunate look, but one that didn't seem racially driven). This left just Yul, Becky Lee, Sundra Oakley, a soft spoken actress, and Ozzy Lusth (page 82) on their Aitu Tribe. What had been an even 6–6 split suddenly tipped into a lopsided 8–4.

But against all odds the Aitu Four proceeded to win every

challenge in thrilling, sweaty upsets, in one of the great underdog stories told on *Survivor*. By the merge, they had narrowed the deficit to four against five.

Still, they were down in numbers. Now came the game changing power of Yul's idol—he would use it as a tool of persuasion, not just a shield for protection. He revealed it to Penner, once an ally, then a traitor, but always a fellow logical thinker. Then he strong-armed Penner with the power of rational thinking: He explained if the Aitu Four all voted for Penner, and Yul successfully used the idol for one of his allies to protect them, Penner would be eliminated. If Penner flipped, he could survive and regain a majority with the Aitu Alliance (Yul thoroughly explained each possible scenario to the self-interested Penner. He shared his thinking—supported by a series of probability equations—in a blog he wrote for friends while the show aired. The math was all there.) This is reflective of Kwon's general approach to strategy on *Survivor*—it was always deeply thought-out, often pulling from game theory and logic. He was "the nerd" after all.

That night, Penner voted with Yul's alliance. The move flipped the season's balance of power and changed how idols would be used forever—not as last-minute lifelines, but as tools of persuasion and narrative control. Now, with the numbers on their side, the Aitu Four held control and slowly eliminated the remaining players (including Penner), to reach the final four.

PART OF THE Aitu's underdog success was Yul's keen strategizing, but another key part of it were **Ozzy Lusth's** impressive performances in the physical challenges. Before the merge, it was with his help that the Aitu were able to win out and never deplete their already-low numbers. In the individual game, he won five of the six Immunity Challenges— tying the record held by Colby Donaldson and others—and giving his Aitu Alliance their pick of the litter on who to eliminate.

Ozzy, who was born in Mexico and originally on the Latino tribe, was a physical contender unlike any before on the show. He wasn't the built, blue collar type of challenger *Survivor* viewers were accustomed to. He was lean and sleek, a jungle boy. Ozzy shimmied up trees to grab coconuts and dove deep to spear fish. He swam and ran and jumped with speed and grace. "Ozzy is amazing. He's like half animal, half man, part fish, part monkey, part lord knows what," his former tribemate (turned mutineer) Candice Woodcock explained. It was as if Ozzy was built to play *Survivor*.

These skills that made him such a strong physical player were reflective of Ozzy's real-life passions. While other players might practice spear fishing or shelter building to prepare for their time on the show, Ozzy did these things for fun, even before he thought about being on *Survivor*. He was a surfer and outdoorsman. He once spent five months camping from Panama to San Diego. Ozzy cites reading *Robinson Crusoe* as a kid as the spark that ignited his love of outdoor adventure. *Survivor*'s concept was based on Robinsonian adventure—the origins of the show were in his blood.

Ozzy's brawn and Yul's brain brought both of them to the finale in *Cook Islands*, along with ally Becky, in *Survivor*'s first three-person Final Tribal. It was one of the most competitive finales in the show's history. As Jeff Probst described: "We have Yul who dominated strategically like maybe nobody else ever has. Ozzy who dominated physically, fair to say, like nobody ever has." And Becky was there too (and in her defense, a great strategic partner during the game, according to Yul).

In the end, Yul's strategic dominance and likability among the jury beat out Ozzy's challenge dominance in a 5–4–0 vote. But Ozzy won the fan favorite vote, in what was also a competitive race between him and Yul.

Ozzy would return three more times. Across those returns, a clear pattern emerged: the challenge beast paradox. In *Cook Islands*, his physicality carried him to the finale, but in every later season it painted a target on his back. Everyone knew the moment Ozzy lost immunity, he should be booted—it might be their only chance.

Whether or not that pattern will hold for his fourth try, coming in 2026's *Survivor 50*, remains to be seen.

Ozzy's greatest gift in *Survivor* is also his biggest liability. As one of the show's most talented competitors, he always has to fight for his safety, but there are few players more suited to do that in *Survivor*'s history than Ozzy Lusth.

YUL KWON SEEMED PERFECT. Or at least to me he did. Yul's visibility was particularly meaningful to me as an Asian American watching at the time, even with his Asian-ness looking very different from mine. Yul's victory mattered not just because he won, but because winning forced his edit to be careful rather than flattened, his story specific rather than symbolic. In 2006, that kind of space was something television rarely afforded Asian American men.

The diversity of *Cook Islands*—even if stuffed in as an ungainly twist—allowed for stories like Yul's, and conversations about the nuances of representation like the one between Yul and Cao Boi. Yul helped shift the lens and became that strong, multidimensional representation he had once longed to see.

After filming ended and the contestants waited for the live reunion to learn the outcome, Yul found himself more anxious about winning than losing. He was worried about the "sudden blast of exposure." In time, this fear became another he was grateful to have confronted. The million-dollar check mattered, of course, but Yul's win came with other life-changing upsides.

For Yul, facing this fear—then coming off thoughtful, strong and decisive—led to changes that lasted long after the game ended. His "fifteen minutes of fame" gave him a larger platform to advocate for bone marrow donations. He met the woman who would become his wife and the mother to his daughters. And, Yul says, his appearance on the show changed his relationship with his father, forever.

Yul's dad was against him being on *Survivor*. He saw Yul as rudderless, jumping from job to job—albeit impressive ones. Yul had to plead with him to sign the waivers necessary for him to play, ultimately only convincing him by saying, "If I go on the show, I'm gonna be seen by thousands of potential Korean wives and their mothers." After the finale, Yul says he heard something he had never heard from his dad before. "He said, 'Yul, I'm sorry. I'm sorry that I doubted you . . . after watching you on *Survivor*, I realized what kind of person you had grown to be, what kind of man you had grown to be. And it is someone I'm really proud of. I love you.'"

Yau-Man Chan

AT THE BEGINNING OF *SURVIVOR: FIJI,* THE SHOW'S FOURTEENTH season airing in 2007, nineteen contestants found themselves together on the one island with no information.[16] This season included the same ratio of diversity as *Cook Islands* before, without the racial segregation.[17]

"Where's Jeff?" the castaways wondered. On cue, a sea plane appeared, with Jeff Probst standing on its edge, like a Tom Cruise stunt. He threw a crate off of the plane and into the water, with a parachute attached, and flew away. The young, strong men rowed out to grab the mysterious wooden box. Back on the beach, they tried smashing it open. The tribe chanted "Rocky, Rocky" as a Stallone lookalike bashed it against a boulder. Others tried dropping the boulder on it, still no luck.

Having seen enough, **Yau-Man Chan** walked up, wagging his finger no. Scrawny, with round glasses and wisps of gray hair, he hardly looked like the one to crack it. But he picked up the crate, dropped it on its corner, and it easily burst open. "It's very simple physics—the weakest point is if you drop it on its corner." As one

16.   One contestant dropped out at the last minute after having a panic attack, leading to this odd number.

17.   It was a move to prove the "race wars" framing wasn't just a one-time stunt for rating. It made for another season filled with textured stories and strong representation, but ultimately not something production would continue to prioritize.

of the oldest and smallest players out there, Yau-Man may not have looked like the typical *Survivor* power player, but he would quickly prove himself to be one of the show's greats—and shape who fans considered a star.

Yau-Man is a computer engineer and table-tennis player from California, but he grew up in Borneo—the filming location of *Survivor*'s first season. With island life in his blood and an instinct to "hack" his way through problems, he became an asset to his team and avoided the fate of early-boot older players deemed too weak by the younger castaways. He outwitted an archery challenge by kneeling to steady his shot, he made fire by angling his glasses like a magnifying lens. Castmates even voted him the person they'd most want to be stranded with. But Yau-Man's most lasting contribution came with the hidden idol.

After receiving the clues on Exile Island, Yau-Man was quickly able to find the idol hidden back at his camp, but then, he decided to take it a step further. "I have a really evil thought," he said. Yau-Man polished and painted a face onto a coconut shell and put the initials "I.I." on it, "just in case they don't know it's an Immunity Idol." He covered the shell in the wrapping his idol came in, and buried it back in the same place. Yau-Man had created the first fake idol shown on *Survivor*. Though no one found the coconut shell, the idea spawned a whole lineage of legendary fakes.

As the show continued, Yau-Man was liked and respected, he had a secret idol, and he was proving to be a fierce competitor in challenges. He also had a strong friendship with Earl Cole, who said, "An older Chinese guy, a young Black guy—friends. Who would have ever thought that? It's like *Rush Hour*." But all of this meant he was becoming the biggest threat to win the game.

With six players left, Yau-Man won a Reward Challenge and with it a brand-new truck. "I want to see if I can make a deal," he told Jeff. In one of the most controversial moments in *Survivor* history, he gave the truck to Dreamz, a formerly homeless contestant who had spoken about not owning a car, in exchange for a promise:

If Dreamz won the final four immunity, he'd give the necklace to Yau-Man. "I promise to God," Dreamz said. The deal was set—Yau-Man sealed it by choosing to send himself to Exile Island, the first player on *Survivor* to ever do so.

That night, as the castaways schemed and strategized in the hours leading up to casting their votes, Yau-Man told Earl, "I have bad vibes." Maybe Dreamz would try to eliminate him before the deal could be fulfilled. With the new rules inspired by Yul, the idol had to be played *before* the votes were read at Tribal Council. Yau-Man followed his gut instinct and played his hidden idol, to the shock of his tribemates; when the votes were read, Yau-Man had, in fact, received the most votes, those of everyone except Earl. He was saved, becoming the first player to successfully use the idol with these new rules.

At the final five, Yau-Man won the Immunity Challenge, a giant maze, and was safe again. At the final four, Dreamz won immunity—time for the truck deal to come through. But Dreamz reneged. He chose not to give up his Immunity Necklace. As the biggest threat to win it all, Yau-Man was voted out, one spot short of Final Tribal. At the reunion, most jurors said Yau-Man would have won.

Instead, Earl won in a unanimous vote, becoming the show's first Black male winner, in the first (and only, thus far) all-Black Final Three. Yau-Man bore no grudge. To Dreamz he said, "The truck was given to you in good faith. Enjoy it. Don't feel guilty." Unsurprisingly, Yau-Man won the fan favorite vote in a landslide.

"Love many. Trust few. Do wrong to none," is how Yau-Man described his *Survivor* gameplan. That philosophy carried him from underestimated underdog to one of the show's most beloved—and most innovative—players. If Rupert Boneham cracked open the door for a *Survivor* hero to depart from Colby Donaldson's Ken-doll archetype, Yau-Man—older, scrawny, Asian—blew that door right off of its hinges. Though he was never called an All-American, he expanded the profile of who could get the hero edit.

Parvati Shallow
& Russell Hantz

IT WAS A HOT, MUGGY MANHATTAN WEEKDAY, BUT THE LINE outside The Strand bookstore snaked all the way around a city block. Sweaty queuers fanned themselves or sat on folding stools, but even on this heavy, humid day, there was a buzz of energy, excited chatter. Everyone was waiting there to see one person: **Parvati Shallow**.

Parvati was signing copies of her new book, *Nice Girls Don't Win*. For over two hours, she greeted each attendee with a kind smile and pleasant small talk, complimenting what they wore or receiving their eager praise with an easy grace. She wore a strapless black dress with white polka dots and black and white Nike Dunks. The line began mostly with men in tight shorts and tank tops—presumably queer men, "my base," she says—but quickly expanded to an array of people: fathers with daughters getting books signed to their wives, older couples, superfans in personalized shirts with Parvati's face on them, young women in University of Georgia hats (Shallow's alma mater). There were attendees who had driven for hours, planned daytrips around the signing or taken the day off from work. Others had already been to previous events on her book tour—like the *Survivor vs. Traitors* themed drag show in Brooklyn the night before, where she took the stage dressed as Boston Rob—but craved another chance to see Parvati in all her glory. Many bought multiple copies of her book. Parvati brought the same warmth and charm to each of the hundreds of fans at the signing over several hours—an impressive feat of social stamina.

There is, perhaps, no other figure in the *Survivor* universe that could drive this kind of excitement and eager awe. Parvati is beloved. "Queen," "Mother,"[18] "Icon," "the greatest of all time," are some of the words used to describe her.

But for Parvati, this outpouring of love is largely new, as recent as the past several years. Viewers have returned to her. Streaming old seasons of *Survivor* lets us watch her trailblazing gameplay in today's context, and her appearances on new shows—like Peacock's *The Traitors*, which fully embraces the flamboyance and duplicity of the genre, in part thanks to her shaping of it—reinforce just how masterful she is.

Parvati is a perfect example of *Survivor* as a mirror of its moment. When she played—primarily between *Cook Islands* in 2007 and *Heroes vs. Villains* in 2010—she was an ice cold strategist and used her feminine charm as a tool in the game. She skewed the gendered expectations of her performance. She was strong and shrewd and observant. Today, those qualities make her an icon of the genre— "mother"—but back then, they made her polarizing. "I am overwhelmingly receiving love these days, which is really cool and really different to how it was when I was younger and playing," Shallow told me over coffee before her book signing. "And it feels like medicine for my younger self."

PARVATI SHALLOW WAS born in an ashram, a commune led by a seemingly omnipotent female guru, Ma Jaya Bhagvati, originally Joyce Green of Brooklyn. In these early years of Parvati's life, she witnessed how Bhagvati would "love bomb" her followers—use intense affection to make them feel safe and loved and dependent— followed by harsh and at times abusive social control. As a child in

---

18. Even the language of her fandom—calling her "mother"—is telling. What was once read as threatening is now celebrated as nurturing leadership, queer-coded charisma, and feminist cunning.

the ashram, Parvati's lifestyle was wild and less structured—running through the lush green of the Florida compound with her pack of fellow devotees' children. Her name, chosen by Bhagvati, comes from the Hindu goddess, Parvati, the goddess of love and beauty—perhaps a prescient decision.

When Shallow's parents escaped the controlling ashram and returned to traditional society, she found she was a hit at school. She was pretty, popular, and powerful. As she writes in her memoir, *Nice Girls Don't Win*: "I thoroughly enjoyed the power that came from being adored without the vulnerability of liking any of the boys back . . . My goals were clear: friendship and social status. I wanted to belong to a tribe of kickass girls. The boys were ancillary symbols of our superior female status." Parvati modeled herself on Buffy (the Vampire Slayer) and Brittany (Spears), beautiful and badass. She was attractive, in the fullest sense of that word—liked for her warmth and spunk by the people in her circle and aspirational for her beauty by those at a distance.

After college, Parvati moved to Los Angeles. "I wanted an adventure. I wanted to be on TV," she tells me. Now, she saw herself in another "B": Brooke Burke. Burke was a model who hosted *Wild on E!*, a travel show in which she—often clad in a skimpy bikini—traveled to popular destinations around the world to report on culture, adventure, and nightlife. Parvati didn't have *Survivor* in mind, she had never watched it, but she was ready for adventure and primed to be a star.

The reality show Shallow did know, and dreamed of competing on, was *The Amazing Race*, another CBS show on which players race around the globe. Someone Parvati knew at the time was involved with casting the *Race*. He asked her if she had a blonde friend she could bring with her for an audition—they'd be the team of young women, a blonde and a brunette (for diversity). Parvati said she had two, her roommates, Julea and Lily. "Great, bring them both," she writes he told her. An audition date was set. Parvati was overjoyed. This could be that big break moment she had been waiting for.

The following week, bubbling with nervous energy, Parvati and her friends entered the Santa Monica hotel where casting interviews took place. They checked themselves in the reflection of the grand elevator's door as they headed up to a penthouse suite. It was time to meet the "goddess" who would control their fate. The three roommates sat on three chairs across from Lynne Spillman, the casting director of *Survivor* fame who was also casting director of *The Amazing Race* at the time. After some initial pleasantries, Lynne looked at Parvati. She told her she could only compete in *The Amazing Race* with one partner. With which friend would she want to play? She had to pick one, now. Parvati looked at her dear friends on either side of her, each just as eager for this opportunity. With just seconds to make a decision, she picked Julea.

"I made her vote one of them out. It was kind of cruel. But that's when I knew she'd be perfect for *Survivor*," Lynne says now.

"She saw something in me," Parvati says of Lynne, who asked her back for the *Survivor* casting process. "I sucked in my casting. I would just get so nervous, I don't even know what I was saying, I'd just be giggling." But between those giggles, there was an evident charm, an alluring quality about Parvati. And a clear ability for cutthroat decisiveness.

Parvati was first cast on *Cook Islands,* the "race wars" season that included Yul Kwon and Ozzy Lusth. She was on the white Rarotonga tribe where, in reaction to the surprising tribe split she said, "Different ethnic groups. I mean, is that kosher?" Parvati knows the archetype she was cast to play as. "I was the hot bikini girl. And it fit me perfectly." She *was* the hot bikini girl, but she would quickly prove that the hot bikini girl could be a brutal force. She knew she was eye candy, but she would flip that male gaze on its head.

While Parvati's strategic legacy would be solidified in later seasons, even on *Cook Islands* she left crumbs of the game-changing gameplay she would come to define. After the tribe swap, she found herself on a tribe with big, buff men. "I'm absolutely going to flirt with them, get them on my good side. It's what I do best," she said with a cheeky smile. "Lure him into my web, chomp him, suck his blood." The Black Widow was being born. In this season, Parvati found herself on the wrong side of the numbers and ultimately couldn't pry that strategic stronghold from Yul. Still, players saw the potential she had as a threat. She was a strong physical player and had a keen power to persuade. In, arguably, her most memorable moment of this first season, Parvati found herself in a hot tub, naked with Yul and Ozzy while the three were on a reward. "Odds were in my favor, I guess," she said wryly. Yul says the whole situation made him incredibly uncomfortable, but he saw the threat Parvati could pose by trying to lure Ozzy to flip on his alliance, so he stuck it out in the hot tub the whole time, making sure he never left the two of them alone.

After *Cook Islands*, Parvati was known as a fun player, but nowhere near the icon she would become. As such, she was shocked when she was called to return three seasons later, reportedly a late replacement for another player who declined. This season, set in Micronesia's Palau Island, was themed *Fans vs. Favorites*.

In the opening scene, the "fans" stood on the beach where they learned who they would be competing against. One-by-one, the "favorite" returning contestants ran out from around a corner. The fans went wild when Yau-Man Chan ran out, with whoops and shouts. They, expectedly, jeered and booed when Jonny Fairplay showed up. When Parvati ran out, there was the requisite polite applause, but to many, this was a curious choice. In her first confessional, we hear Parvati acknowledge her reputation: "I was a flirt in *Cook Islands* and that was it. Like, there was no other dimension to me at all I don't think. Outwardly I'm still going to be flirty, but I'm playing smart this time."

Shallow had come prepared for this second chance. "I'm not here to starve and not win," she remembers telling a producer. She was strong as ever, working professionally as a boxer in LA. But more importantly she came ready to play an "ice cold" game. She had read *The Rules of Persuasion* and *The 48 Laws of Power*—"which is a psycho book." She gave herself permission to "slit your throat before you get me." She says she's normally the type of person who, if a deer is bleeding out, would try to give it a tourniquet and take it to the hospital. For this game, she knew, "I'm gonna have to stomp the deer in the head."

There was a heartlessness that Parvati was allowing herself to access. It can be a successful path to victory (not dissimilar to the game of a Richard Hatch or Boston Rob), but it is a hard place to go, and harder still for female contestants who are expected (by society, the show, and the audience) to play with more compassion. This understanding led to another important decision Parvati made going into the game: she wanted to get to the end with all women. "I've seen the men get preferential treatment. Simply because they're men, they're seen to be better in challenges, they're seen to be more strategic players," she tells me. "I was like, no chance I'm letting a man get to the end. There's gonna be an even playing field for me to win. There has to be all women."

With this clear goal and a new ice queen mentality, Parvati was ready to play what would become one of the most memorable winning games in *Survivor* history—and inaugurate a cutthroat path to success that no female player had been allowed to successfully pull off.

To do this, she knew she had to first return to form and be underestimated as *just* the "hot bikini girl." In the pre-merge, she connected with James Clement, a gravedigger and fan-favorite from the previous season, *Survivor: China*, who was one of the brawniest players the show had seen. Together with Ozzy, who found himself infatuated with the doe-eyed Amanda Kimmel, a former Miss Montana and *Survivor: China* finalist, the foursome formed a Couples Alliance.

Flirtation clearly came naturally to Shallow, but it would be amiss to consider it haphazard; she knew exactly what she was doing. Drawing people in with her smile, a light touch, and easy confidence was one arrow in Parvati's growing strategic quiver—one she aimed with increasing precision. She always knew she would have to drop James and Ozzy eventually, but it certainly didn't hurt to cozy up to the strongest men in the game—figures who often think they're in control early (and who can provide a nice big spoon for cool Pacific nights).

Quickly, she amassed power. During a tribe swap, Parvati connected with two young women originally on the Fans team, Natalie Bolton and Alexis Jones. When Cirie Fields (page 105), a nurse and *Survivor* legend in her own right, proposed taking out Ozzy, Shallow was ready to turn on the Couples. Her social ease disguised the plan; she made Ozzy feel protected. He was blindsided at Tribal Council later that night with a hidden idol in his pocket.

The next day, Parvati had to smooth things over with Amanda and James. James, who was often quick with a biblical allusion, said with frustration: "You always gotta eat the apple. You can't just leave the apple alone and just enjoy." But what James didn't see in this Micronesian Garden of Eden was that Parvati had bitten the apple before she even arrived. She was never playing an innocent game.

Along with Cirie, Natalie and Alexis, and a newly integrated Amanda, Parvati became the face of *Survivor*'s most memorable alliance. "It's like the Black Widow Brigade. All the girls are coming together and we're spinning the guys around as much as we can, just spinning them and spinning them until they don't know which way is up. And then we're devouring them, one at a time," Parvati explained. They stirred their imaginary witch's cauldron with a gleeful cackle.

The Black Widow Brigade eliminated almost every man from the game—with Parvati winning challenges along the way and outsmarting other players who had hidden idols—until there was only one left: Erik Reichenbach, a Michigan ice cream scooper with a surfer's mop of blonde hair and naive blue eyes. The issue: He kept winning immunity. In one of the all-time moves in *Survivor* history, the Black Widow Brigade manipulated Erik into giving up his Immunity Necklace—his safety—and promptly voted him out. "You're crazy. You'll officially go down as the dumbest Survivor ever, in the history of *Survivor*. Ever," Parvati said at the voting booth.

Parvati made it to the final two with her dear friend and closest ally, Amanda. She had done what she set out to do, in almost flawless fashion. She used her charm and allure to manipulate. She turned on allies and slit throats with precision. She got to the final four with all women—the first time in the show's history this was done, with any gender. Shallow won challenges and outsmarted her opponents. "With the help of a group of powerful women, we pulled off some of the greatest heists in *Survivor* history," she told the jury at Final Tribal. They had. Still, many on the jury, particularly the men, were bitter.

Ozzy—in a speech that had none of the pizzazz but all of the resentment of Sue Hawk's (page 21) snakes and rats speech—turned to Parvati at the Final Tribal Council and said: "I never, in a million years, thought you could do that to me. You put a price on our friendship; you threw us away like garbage!" Shallow opened her mouth to reply, but Ozzy continued, "I don't want words, no words at all. I don't want to talk to you." He would go on to tell Amanda he was "starting to fall in love" with her. Ozzy reportedly had a girlfriend at the time and later, allegedly, cheated on Amanda—yet that did nothing to temper the anger he held for Parvati over *her* "betrayal," choosing a million dollars over their friendship. Ozzy's heartbreak wasn't just personal—it was cultural. The show's men could outwit and be praised; a woman who did the same was accused of betrayal.

Parvati won the game, 5-3. She received the votes of all of the women on the jury, plus one man, gymnast Jason Siska. Amanda received the votes of the men scorned: Ozzy, James, and Erik.

Amanda also played a fantastic but more understated, social game. She played a role not dissimilar to female winners of the past—like Tina Wesson, Vecepia Towery, and Sandra Diaz-Twine. It was a quieter game, one of knowingly letting the male egos around you shine bright and burn out, of slipping through and downplaying your own strategic moves. It is a really smart way to play *Survivor*, especially among those big ego players.

But Parvati did something new: She broke a glass ceiling. She played with a loud femininity. She played with the ice cold strategy and physical prowess that made many men heroes of the game, but she did something more. Parvati took the Jerri Manthey-esque temptress role expected of her by her fellow players and production and used it to her advantage. She blew the gates of how to win *Survivor* as a woman wide open.

But this game-changing approach wasn't widely celebrated at the time. "I felt very vilified after I played the second time," Parvati says now. "Especially by Ozzy, who was a friend of mine . . . when he was really personally hurt and attacking me, it really landed." Despite being a million dollars richer, it was that hate that she felt from Ozzy, and later the press and viewers, that really impacted Parvati. She was called a "slut" and a "vapid whore" for using flirtation to advance herself in the game. And she internalized it. "I didn't have a strong sense of self developed at the time. I was very young, I didn't have a career path, I didn't have any sense of what I was doing with my life . . . So those comments just seeped in, and they altered how I felt about myself," she says. "I thought I was someone who would manipulate or take advantage of other people to get ahead in life, because I'd done that in the game and I didn't have any clear boundary between game and reality . . . it definitely seeped into my psyche, and I was kind of swirling around in some chaos for many years."

It was in this mindset that Parvati played again, just two years later, on *Survivor*'s twentieth season, *Heroes vs. Villains* (as a villain, of course). Here, she would align herself with *Survivor*'s most notorious villain ever: "I definitely feel like I'm making a deal with the devil. But I want the devil on my side."

ON THE FIRST night of *Survivor*'s nineteenth season, set in Samoa, **Russell Hantz** told his tribemates the harrowing and tragic story of his experience during Hurricane Katrina. Muddy water came gushing into his house, rising quickly. As a fireman, he grabbed his axe, wanting to help his neighbors, but first had to escape upstairs. Then he turned, calling for his beloved German Shepherd, Rocky. As he looked back, he saw Rocky being swept away, swallowed by the muddy waters. A heart-breaking moment that shaped him forever, he said.

Later, he told the cameras: "I never lived in New Orleans, I'm not a fireman, I've never even had a German Shepherd. It's crazy how you can break their hearts by telling them a lie." It was just the first night, and Russell was throwing around Jonny Fairplay-level lies just for the fun of it. And he was testing the waters of how much emotional manipulation he could get away with.

Russell was a Texas oil company owner. He made clear from the get-go, he wasn't playing for the money. He was only there to prove "how easy it is to win this game," if you're willing to go far enough. He's short, round, and bald with a goatee and signature fedora. Or, as perhaps best described by Courtney Yates, the one-liner queen from *Survivor: China* and the "beans" to Sandra Diaz-Twine's "rice" in *Heroes vs. Villains*: "He's like a bandy-legged little troll who scampers around with his tooth missing, and is in and out of the bushes and never washes."

Russell was plainly there to manipulate, lie, and brute force his way to the end. "I plan on making it as miserable as possible, making it hell for everybody, to get what I want," he explained. On that same first night as he told the Katrina story, he burned his tribemates' socks and poured out all the water in their canteens just for the sake of creating chaos and misery. "I figure if I can control how they feel, I can control how they think."

This worked. Russell made alliances with almost all of the women on his tribe: "My strategy is to have a secret alliance with each one of these dumb girls. I like to call it my dumb-ass girl alliance." His tribe, because of the misery and sabotage he was stirring up, consistently lost challenges, but this played to Russell's advantage. They were going to Tribal Council every episode, and anyone who questioned him or expressed uncertainty would be voted out. "You can call me the puppet master," he boasted. "They're my little puppets. They'll run when I tell them to run, they'll walk when I tell them to walk. When I'm finished with them, I'll just throw them in the trash."

Russell brought a new level of cruelty to the game, but also a new level of gameplay. Perhaps most notably, he was the first player to find a Hidden Immunity Idol without a clue. Russell deeply craved to be considered a great, to be inducted into the game's mythology: a king of the game. He realized, "If I could find that idol, that would be genius. In the history of *Survivor*, how many people found the idol without a clue? Zero." He scuttled around, looking near landmarks—oddly shaped trees, the water well, under the bridge—and eventually found the idol, buried among the roots of a notable tree near their camp. Russell knew production would have hidden an idol, and he found it just like that, with no clues leading him to it. He had just outsmarted the game.

At the merge, Russell played his idol. Then he found another the very next day, enforcing this idea of his seeming omnipotence among the fellow castaways. Since Russell, idol searches without clues have become commonplace.

With this authority of power, and the lack of any line too far to cross, Russell brute forced his way to the finale with one of the "dumb blondes" with whom he aligned himself early, Southern belle Natalie White. "She's going to ride my coattails the entire way. She's too stupid to do it by herself. She needs me," he said. But Natalie—a deeply underedited character in a season with so much time devoted to Russell's merciless maneuverings—understood her game. In one of the few strategic moments we get to hear from her, she said she wanted to remain underestimated and loyal so that Russell would take her to the end. And while he was rubbing everyone the wrong way, she would build strong relationships, ensuring the jury would like her more than him.

Going into the Final Tribal with Natalie and the hunky but "feckless" LA doctor named like a soap opera character—Mick

Trimming—Russell was confident. "My work is done. It's like a painting, like a Picasso. He's a great artist; this is my artwork. This is one of my best pieces of work I've ever done. And it's going to be a pretty expensive sale; they'll write me a check for a million dollars for this work." Also like Picasso, he was an arrogant misogynist.

Before the Season 19 reunion, where the final votes were read and Russell could "confirm" the win he was confident he had in the bag, he returned to Samoa to film *Heroes vs. Villains*. Sandra Diaz-Twine recalls him asking her details about when and how she received her million-dollar check. Russell knew he had won one season, and was here to take another.

Season 19 hadn't yet aired, so his fellow players on *Heroes vs. Villains* hadn't yet witnessed his antics. They were just told by production that he was "one of the five most notorious male villains of all time."

Instead, there was another player whose villainous legacy loomed large over this twentieth season of all-stars.

BY THE TIME of *Heroes vs. Villains* in 2010, *Survivor* wasn't just testing endurance—it was testing who gets to be powerful on television.

Parvati Shallow entered *Heroes vs. Villains* as a huge target. In pregame interviews, several players identified her as the biggest threat. She was a calculated and strategic player, a temptress who could sway minds with her witchy magic. She had just won one of the most dominant, impressive games in recent history. The looming legacy of the Black Widow and her powerful Brigade would shape this season.

With few players willing to align with her, Parvati made her "deal with the devil" and aligned with Russell Hantz, as well as Danielle DiLorenzo, a *Survivor: Panama* finalist. Her fellow villains were leery. Boston Rob and Benjamin "Coach" Wade warned Russell that Parvati was a dangerous player he should avoid. Even before the first vote, she was framed, her game too dangerous.

In Russell's warped mind, he may have believed he had found

himself another beautiful, blindly loyal, "dumb girl," subject to his reign of terror, but to Parvati, she was the one calling the shots. She was building another web, and it seems like Russell was caught in it. As she writes in *Nice Girls Don't Win*: "While others bowed in fear or protested against him, I found I could easily negotiate my relationship with him by throwing him little nuggets of validation here and there. I called him my hero and gave him sweet hugs. The cheap sugar seemed a small price to pay to make it to the end of the game." It was emotional aikido: using validation to redirect aggression.

When Utah cyclist Tyson Apostol (page 119) misread a split-vote plan, Parvati and Russell seized control, and their minority alliance was able to pick off the others: Tyson, then Boston Rob, then Coach. The Heroes, meanwhile, watched from their camp as the men fell one by one. They imagined a Black Widow resurrection. Alabama cattle rancher J.T. Thomas (page 127) was convinced another "all-devouring female alliance" was forming. He feared Parvati would bring her witchy ways to the merge.

Hoping to play hero, J.T. made one of the most infamous (read: stupid) moves in *Survivor* history.[19] At a challenge, he slipped the notorious Russell Hantz an idol with a note telling him to use it to cut Parvati. "Just by competing against you and the few handshakes we've had, I feel like I can trust you," it read. Russell, delighted, showed the note to Parvati, and they laughed together—but with that laugh came insight. J.T. saw Russell as an ally; Parvati saw proof that at the merge she would once again be the top target.

Come merge, the Heroes' contempt for Parvati was obvious. "They don't know it yet," Parvati said, "but they're about to be picked off one by one." Again she was right. Shallow now held two idols—her own and J.T.'s—which Russell promptly handed over, his latest tribute to her control. At Tribal, she played neither for

19. In fact, it even beat Erik giving up his necklace in a "Stupidest Move in *Survivor* History" fan vote at the reunion of this season.

herself. Instead, she saved Sandra and Jerri, sending J.T. home by his own idol.

Before exiting, J.T. shook Russell's hand and said "well done," despite Hantz having nothing to do with this move. In his exit interview he said: "This is probably one of the biggest moves in *Survivor* history and it did not go in my favor. I know that people are villains for a reason, don't ever trust them. Worse than that, don't ever trust women. Ever, ever, ever."

With Parvati winning them control, the Villains picked off the Heroes, just as she had predicted. She also dominated in challenges, winning three, even against players who had been considered challenge greats like Colby Donaldson and Rupert Boneham.

At the Final Tribal Council, with Russell and Sandra, Parvati touted her challenge success and her many impressive strategic moves, getting to the end despite being the biggest target from the beginning. But it wasn't enough to convince the jury. They only saw Parvati as an extension of Russell.

"You played this game under Russell's thumb the whole time, like a spouse in a bad, abusive relationship. And you never got out of it," *Cook Islands* mutineer Candice Woodcock told Shallow. "I like you, but I can't support that." But was Parvati under his thumb? Or was Russell under hers? She was the one shaping the vote, charming her way into being given his idols, winning challenges. She was the architect, the strategist. But Russell was loud, emoting and projecting dominance, if never really earning it. He was the one getting the handshakes (and lots of the screen time). He was the man.

RUSSELL WOULD GO to his reunion for *Survivor: Samoa* and find out he had lost 7-2-0 to his "dumb girl" ally Natalie White. He only got two votes. He was a sore loser: "I don't think she deserves it," he said. Months later, he would get zero votes in the finale of his second competition, losing to both Sandra and Parvati at the reunion for *Heroes vs. Villains* in the 6-3-0 result that made Queen Sandra the first two-time winner.

If Richard Hatch proved some ruthlessness was essential to win *Survivor*, Russell Hantz exposed its limits. Juries wouldn't reward his cruelty—but audiences seemed to eat it up. Russell won the fan favorite vote on both of these seasons, beating out beloved favorites of a previous era like Rupert and Colby. In just ten years, viewers had come a long way since Hatch became a pariah for his (comparably tame) antics. Across reality TV, villains were increasingly celebrated for the drama they created, while antiheroes like *Breaking Bad's* Walter White were taking over popular culture. And yet, the sharply different responses to Russell's cruelty and Parvati's dominance suggested there were still limits to what a celebrated villain could look like.

SANDRA WAS A deserving winner; Parvati would have been one as well. But between the backlash she received after her first game and the way she was misunderstood in the second, Parvati grew to understand something fundamental about this show. "There is definitely a difference in how men and women are treated in life, and it is no different on *Survivor*," she says. "It's a survival show, which already is inherently masculine. So it leans in that direction. The majority of the people on the production are men. The host is a man; his circle, it's mostly men. So of course that is going to play a part in how the show is made and produced and edited . . . There is a filter on the lens."

Parvati's arc—from the "hot bikini girl" to one of the show's most formidable strategic and physical forces—shows how that lens can shift, or more precisely, how a player can seize it and refocus it herself. She never stopped being the "hot bikini girl"; instead, she performed the role with a wink, turning it into part of her strategy. Shallow mastered the campy acknowledgement, blurring the line between character and gameplay—and in doing so, redefining what power could look like on *Survivor*. Parvati was ahead of her time, and she paid for it—facing ridicule and hostility for pairing the strategic aggression men were celebrated for with a femininity she refused to mute. But now audiences can look back and appreciate the full brilliance of her game.

"The wheel keeps turning. You can be on top and then on the bottom," Parvati says, reflecting on her *Survivor* career. "That is the *Survivor* experience: The tide can change in an instant. You're confident in the morning and then you're . . . at Tribal Council, getting your torch snuffed. Life is not unlike that."

More recently, Parvati found herself on top again. Playing on Australia's popular version of *Survivor* in 2025, a season that brought together top players from around the globe, Parvati was at her peak. She was again an early target, she again played closely aligned with Cirie, she again was charming, strategically savvy, and dominant in physical challenges. This time, Shallow won. This win, against some of the world's best players, drove discussion that she may truly be the greatest to ever play this weird little game.

Some may have missed the genius of Parvati back in *Cook Islands* when she was flirting in the hot tub with Ozzy and Yul, but today, no one can overlook her. Shallow is beloved. An icon, mother, and queen, and perhaps the greatest *Survivor* player of all time. She shaped the game and changed how female strategists are perceived. And she looked damn good doing it.

Cirie Fields

THE CROWN OF "BEST TO NEVER WIN" IS A HARD ONE TO WEAR.
It's heavy and jagged, woven with "what-ifs" and "if onlys." It's not
the dazzled two-win tiara of Queen Sandra Diaz-Twine, nor the
dark, twisted headpiece of the Black Widow, Parvati Shallow, but it
is a crown that **Cirie Fields** wears with grace.

As Parvati turned flirtation lethal, Cirie wielded a different kind
of charm. Cirie Fields transformed "likability" from a personality
trait into one of the game's most effective strategic weapons.

Fields first appeared on the show's twelfth season, *Survivor:
Panama—Exile Island*, in 2006.[20] But she was an unexpected player
on *Survivor*. Casting director Lynne Spillman remembers reading
her application and thinking, "She doesn't even want to do this."
Then she watched Cirie's video from an open call. In it, Fields reit-
erated: "Don't pick me. I don't want to do it." Instead, she was advo-
cating for her sister, Cicely. But Lynne says the video was hilarious.
She was laughing when Executive Producer Mark Burnett walked
by. "I just got one," she told him. "He was like, 'What do you mean?
She doesn't even want to be on the show.'" Lynne insisted, "Trust
me. She's really good. She's going to be a star." Again, Spillman
was right.

---

20. Aptly named, it was the first season to, in a significant way, include the
twist of an Exile Island—an isolated island where a player could be sent, suffer-
ing the elements and loneliness for a day or two with no companions and minimal supplies. It also often hid the Immunity Idol (or a clue to it).

In this season, one before *Cook Islands*'s race wars, original tribes were split up by age and gender: older men, younger men, older women, younger women. At thirty-five, Cirie found herself on the older women's tribe. "Whoa, whoa, whoa. I'm on the wrong team! Why do they think I'm older? Do I look older?" she said. Cirie was immediately funny, engaging TV. She was also a fish out of water. She had never slept outdoors and wasn't a fan of it. Famously, she was scared of leaves—or, more accurately, of clearing leaves because of what might be living underneath them.

She may not have been a natural at the survival part of the game, but she quickly proved she was exceptional at the social game. After the "older" women lost the first Immunity Challenge, Cirie's head was on the chopping block as the least helpful with survival skills, but she was able to convince her tribemates—likely against their best interest—to instead target Tina Scheer, a lumberjill who was a workhorse at camp. It didn't really make sense, but such was the power of Cirie Fields.

At that first Tribal, Cirie said the *Survivor* experience was more difficult than she could have anticipated. "For the people at home that are like me on the couch, stay on the couch." Production used this line to paint her as *Survivor*'s everywoman. "The woman who got up off the couch and played *Survivor*," as Jeff put it. She was relatable—and in turn, became one of the biggest fan favorites ever on the show. But the "everywoman" isn't her biography; Fields is quite exceptional. She is a mother of three and an operating room nurse, often working in the ICU. The everywoman tag helped make her relatable, but it also made her remarkable success seem accidental, her strategy instinctive rather than intellectual. But Cirie isn't just anyone.

Cirie has a magnetic quality, a likability that shines so bright it blinds her fellow players to her often-treacherous strategic play. At the merge, she led the effort to eliminate Nick Stanbury, a strong physical threat from the opposing alliance. Still, when he was voted out, he threw his socks back, specifying they were for Cirie—a valuable parting gift in a game where socks get wet and winds blow cold, and one he happily gave to his executioner.

Cirie's most impressive strategic move of the game, one that put her on the map and would be emulated in the future, came at the final six, where she pulled off the first intentional 3-2-1 vote.

Cirie had found herself in the middle of a collapsing alliance. Two players were targeting one person, and three were targeting another. She could have simply picked a side—but instead, she built her own. Zeroing in on Courtney Marit, a caustic fire dancer others wanted to drag to the end as a "goat," Cirie quietly re-wired the plan. In a signature, historic move, Cirie approached her tribemates separately in the hours leading up to Tribal Council, convincing the people in danger to vote together with her and save themselves. She knew exactly where every vote was going and used that knowledge to engineer a *plurality*, not a majority: three votes for Courtney, two for one target, one for the third. That night, Courtney went home. Cirie understood math, but also people—and how to influence them.

The 3-2-1 vote wasn't just clever arithmetic. It was proof that emotional intelligence could function as strategic power. Cirie replaced brute alliance with soft governance; she created a new category of power where influence was invisible, and control could sound like kindness.

This season, Fields almost made it to the final four, and would have had a good shot at winning, but she was eliminated in a tie-breaking fire-making challenge. Her lack of survival skills came back to bite her, and she just couldn't get her flame big enough.

Cirie then returned two years later for *Fans vs. Favorites* in Micronesia. Again she gained power by playing straight down the middle. On one side was the Couples Alliance with Parvati and Amanda and their respective island flings. On the other side was Jonathan Penner, Yau-Man Chan, Eliza Orleans, and Ami Cusack. Both alliances were vying for Cirie's tie-breaking number. "I think they could do a little more for me, actually," Cirie joked. "No one is washing my clothes; I haven't gotten any special meals . . . I should probably be carried, like on a chariot type thing."

Eventually, Cirie sided with the Couples Alliance in exchange for the guaranteed loyalty of Amanda and Parvati until the end: "I have both of you guys' words that it's us three to the end? I don't care if James proposes to you or you and Ozzy have little Ozlets." They agreed, setting the foundation for the Black Widow Brigade.

At the merge, Cirie became the essential strategic mind behind the Brigade, the mafia boss who had her dirty work done for her. She orchestrated the blindsides of Ozzy, and later Jason Siska, instructing Natalie Bolton on how to make him feel safe.

When it came time for the iconic final spinning of the web, gaslighting Erik Reichenbach into giving up the Immunity Necklace, Fields was the mastermind. "I wonder if he would give Nat his necklace?" she asked. She told Natalie, "Tell him that if he were to give you the necklace, that would redeem him and we would vote for Amanda." She encouraged Amanda and Parvati to "blast" Erik at Tribal Council, that move Parvati pulled off with perfection.

The way the Black Widow Brigade executed their plan—the spinning and tossing, and ultimate devouring of Erik—is almost scary to watch. And Cirie was the spider that knew just where to place each strand of a deadly web to catch her unwitting prey. At Tribal, Erik, exasperated by the allegations he was playing both sides (God forbid the poor man strategize!), announced: "It was stupid, it was just a mistake! I feel like I need to come to Tribal tonight and ask for some sense of forgiveness." Cirie responded: "I think you are able to redeem yourself . . . If you've been discredited, the words you say mean absolutely nothing, it's your actions that will show and prove what's really going on." This was the final word, the nail in the coffin, the devouring of the prey. "I know that actions do speak louder than words," Erik said. "I want to give individual immunity to Natalie."

As she placed her vote to eliminate him, Cirie said, "My mother always told me, you may not be able to beat 'em with these all the time" pointing to her biceps, "but you can always beat 'em with this," pointing to her brain.

Once again, Fields was behind one of the biggest strategic moves in the game's history. Once again, she was well-placed to win it all, and once again, she would fall just short.

Parvati, Amanda, and Cirie stuck to their plan. They got to the end together. But Jeff Probst had one final announcement: Because of the medical evacuations this season, only two players would move to the finals.

It was a stab to the heart. As Amanda put it, in tears, "When is it going to end? There's only so much you can take. Someone has to leave now? After everything? I am so tight with these girls." But between those tears, Amanda stuck with her original coupled ally, Parvati. Cirie fell just short. As the last member on the jury, she voted for Parvati to win. Game recognizing game.

Cirie played again for *Heroes vs. Villains* but was eliminated in the fourth episode. She was well-positioned on her Heroes tribe, but J.T. (clearly on a witch hunt against anything that resembled the Black Widow Brigade) flipped his vote and encouraged firefighter Tom Westman to use an idol to save himself, blindsiding Cirie.

Fields returned a fourth time in *Game Changers* in 2017, more than a decade after her first appearance. The title promised evolution—an all-star class of players who had rewritten the rules. But by this point *Survivor* itself had changed too. The game was now an arms race of idols, advantages, and twists. In its earliest seasons, Cirie's gift— the ability to read people—was the purest form of power. By *Game Changers*, that power was at risk.

Still, she adapted. The biggest names coming into that season— Tony Vlachos, Sandra Diaz-Twine, Ozzy Lusth—were eliminated early, undone by overplaying their reputations. Cirie, as always, found the middle, building webs of connection so that information flowed to her from all sides. She spoke different dialects of trust to different players: to Midwest cop Sarah Lacina, she got down to brass tacks and skipped the small talk; to the sensitive Tai Trang (page 149), she was slow and warm; to strategist Aubry Bracco, she traded logic for logic.

In one of the season's most revealing scenes, Cirie pulled aside Michaela Bradshaw, a fiery, young player who was seen by many on her tribe as aggressive. "You're a very smart girl," Cirie told her. "You have to control your emotions. If you're hungry, get un-hungry; if you're mad, get un-mad." Filling in at confessional, she added: "When I was Michaela's age, I was a hothead like Michaela, I thought I knew everything. But I've learned when you put that guard up, you push people away, and in a game like *Survivor*, you want to bring as many people in as possible." It was mentorship, but also confession— the distilled version of how Cirie herself had learned to survive. For years she'd been performing calm, good humor, and grace: traits that kept her in the game but also kept her readable to a mostly white audience. Her advice to Michaela, also Black, wasn't about manners; it was about self-preservation—control yourself before they decide you've lost control of the story.

Later, that contrast—the difference between domination and empathy—played out in miniature. Brad Culpepper, a former NFL player, had won immunity. Back at the beach, he sat down Tai Trang, a gentle gardener who had found two hidden idols, and told him his ally Aubry was going home, demanding Tai hand the idols over. "I won't want any funny business."

"He made me feel like a dog," Tai said later. Cirie approached Tai differently. "I know Tai, after everything, it's hard for you to trust me. I understand that. However, if we don't do anything, they're going to just pick us off, one-by-one." She apologized to him for the past betrayals and asked to work together to decide who to vote out. Her approach worked. They would vote together, but ultimately it wouldn't matter.

That night, five advantages collided: two idols from Tai who saved himself and Aubry, a Legacy Advantage saving Sarah, an idol from Troyzan, and Brad's Immunity Necklace. Everyone laughed at this wild turn of events, but a hesitant Cirie was counting in her head, starting to understand what this meant. As Jeff explained, "Any votes cast for Tai, Aubry, Sarah, Troyzan will not count. You could not vote for Culpepper, he had immunity. Which means, Cirie, it doesn't matter what votes are in the urn, because the only person who could receive votes . . . " "Is me," Cirie finished, realizing what this meant. "And for what it's worth, not a single vote in here has your name on it," Jeff added. It was another historic moment that Cirie was a part of—the most idols ever played, the most people ever safe at a Tribal Council, and the first person voted out "simply because there is no other choice." Without receiving any of the votes, Cirie had been eliminated, once again just short of the prize. The player who had once defined *Survivor*'s social intelligence was undone by its twists. Fields hadn't been outplayed; she'd been outproduced.

It was an emotional departure for one of the game's most legendary figures. "This has been one of the most grand experiences of my life," Cirie said with a laugh in her voice and a tear rolling down her cheek. "It changed me. I would have never done any of this stuff if I didn't get off that couch eleven years ago. I would have never met so many different people, I would have never had so many amazing experiences. So, it's bittersweet, however, I'm going out in grand style." She left with a standing ovation from the jury.

Cirie's departure felt like more than a loss—it was a moment that exposed an overcorrection. The show she'd helped mature had muddied past that old experiment about human nature, past her ability to charm her way to safety. And to many, it had gone too far.

In the years since, Cirie has carried her legacy beyond *Survivor*, cowinning USA Network's *Snake in the Grass* and becoming the inaugural winner of Peacock's *The Traitors*. When survival skills and physical advantages fell away, her intelligence finally got its due. Yet on *Survivor* itself, fortune has remained fickle. In *Australia vs. The World*, she reached the final four, only to lose in a fire-making challenge again. She'll return once more for *Survivor 50*, still chasing the one title that has eluded her.

Fields wears the heavy crown of the best player to never win—another coronation-cum-canonization. In *Survivor*'s teenaged seasons (often considered to be the "Golden Era"), players like Cirie, Parvati, and Yul reshaped the idea of what a threatening strategist could look like. Parvati and Cirie accepted the archetypes the show assigned them, but proved exceptional within them—the seductress as tactician, the woman just "off the couch" as master strategist. They showed that strategic mastery could excel, no matter production's framing of character.

Their success opened a new phase of the show: players who would not just inhabit archetypes, but stretch them, complicate them, and sometimes reject them entirely. The *Survivor* story was no longer just about who could adapt to the game's rules—it became about who could rewrite their role within the show's growing mythology.

CHAPTER 4

Dragon Slayers and Super Nerds

The Meta Game

Benjamin Wade
& Tyson Apostol

IN THE MIST-CLOAKED HILLS OF KNOXVILLE, TENNESSEE, A legend was born. A man beyond men. A figure destined for glory: the Dragon Slayer. The truest of Renaissance Men—coach, conductor, noble warrior—he wears many masks, yet each one reveals the same unshakable core. "Unbreakable, unbending, unmoving, immeasurable, immovable, invincible," he has faced many a foe, stared death in the face "five, six, seven, or eight" times. He has overcome the blustering winds of a hurricane and attacks by the fiercest of animals. Even in solitude, trials find him. Upon the mighty Amazon—vast, endless, treacherous—he dared to paddle alone, as only the bravest could. But the shadows were watching. Indigenous hunters, standing "four, four and a half feet tall," captured him and hog tied him. They beat him with clubs, and he sensed their cannibalistic hunger, "looking at [his] ass, talking about eating [his] ass." Yet no bonds could hold him. By cunning and by might, he tore free, and for days wrestled with the serpentine waters until he emerged, unbroken, unconquered, "unbreakable, unbending, unmoving, immeasurable, immovable, invincible." He is the keeper of integrity. He is the vessel of truth. He "kind of started the samurai thing." His footsteps fall not on mere soil, but upon the eternal path of the noble warrior. He is the Dragon Slayer.

"WHO IS THIS JACKASS?" make-up artist Erinn Lobdell asked while one of her castmates "conducted" Tchaikovsky's *Marche Slave* to an audience of his confused, irritated tribe, waving his hands around grandly with no music to be found.

This "jackass" is **Benjamin "Coach" Wade**: the Dragon Slayer. Or, it's who he thinks he is. Or who he *wants us to think* he thinks he is. Truth is a convoluted thing when it comes to Coach.

Coach played his first game on *Survivor: Tocantins*, airing in 2009 and set in the vast, dramatic orange sands of the Brazilian highlands. He has shoulder length hair, often adorned with a feather. He "looks like the love child between Steven Seagal and the *Last of the Mohicans*," as his tribemate Tyson Apostol put it.

It is true that Coach is, in fact, a soccer coach—hence the name— and a part-time symphony conductor in Northern California— hence the flair for performance. Whether he was actually captured and beaten by short, cannibalistic locals on a record-setting kayak trip down the Amazon River, as he claims, is harder to confirm. Another tricky detail to verify: He says he learned Chongg Ran, the Tai Chi–like martial art he practices on *Survivor*—to the editors' delight, who scored his movements with sweeping music and shots of birds in flight—from monks in a remote Tibetan monastery, where the form is said to be passed down only by oral tradition. "You can't even Google it," he said on the show.

When you do (inevitably) Google it, Chongg Ran appears only in a spy-thriller book series. Another delusion? Perhaps. But the authors claim their inspiration came from "a remote corner of Chinese-occupied Tibet" where it is passed down "only through oral instruction."[21] Maybe, just maybe, Coach is telling the truth after all.

But the truth almost doesn't matter. Because Coach's version of the truth made for great TV.

---

21. A Reddit user on r/Survivor traced "Chongg Ran" to the Pendergast series by Douglas Preston and Lincoln Child. In a message board about the books, a commenter reported that Preston responded to a reader inquiry sharing the origins of the martial art in their book—a strikingly similar story to the one Coach tells.

———

THE FIRST FIFTEEN seasons of Survivor didn't see many castaways returning to play again. They had *All-Stars* in Season 8 with top players returning, and Season 11 brought back two fan favorites from the previous season, but outside of those exceptions, it wasn't an expectation. Parvati Shallow says that when she was asked back for *Fans vs. Favorites* she was shocked, not just because she didn't think she had yet earned the "favorite" moniker, but also because she didn't even realize that playing again was an option. But after *Fans vs. Favorites*—and perhaps thanks to its success—practically every other season through the 20s and 30s featured returning players in some form—16, 20, 22, 23, 25, 26, 27, 31, 34, 38 and 40.

Now there was a new way to be successful on *Survivor*. You didn't have to win—you just had to make for good enough TV to be asked back.

And Coach made for good TV. After *Tocantins,* he played on *Heroes vs. Villains,* announcing that "this time, I slay everyone and trust no one." But he became the mocked nobleman—his righteousness clashed with Sandra Diaz-Twine's bluntness, his claim to honor was upstaged by Russell Hantz's viciousness. Coach was made the fool.

He returned a third time for the twenty-third season, *Survivor: South Pacific,* vowing to control his "sense of self-righteousness and judgement on the others." This did him well. *South Pacific* featured Coach and Ozzy Lusth each returning to play on a team of newbies.[22] Players were thrilled to see Ozzy, hoping to have the jungle-boy on their team, and expressly disappointed to see Coach, saying "he's just going to be so loony and out there, he's just going to be nuts." Instead, Coach helped lead a competitive

22. The same format was used the season before with Russell Hantz and Boston Rob each leading a tribe. Russell was voted out first while Rob ended up winning the season.

team and a dominant alliance post-merge (albeit with a cult-like mentality and lots of prayer), while Ozzy came off as a "lazy ass . . . arrogant jungle boy" in the estimation of tribemate John Cochran (page 129).

Coach made it to the finale this season, but finished in second place, losing to witty med student Sophie Clarke in a 6-3-0 vote. At Final Tribal Council, he was unable to escape his own narrative that he had played an "honorable game," which doesn't land with a jury you've played a role in eliminating. He returns, once more, for *Survivor 50.*

A moment that really revealed Coach—where we saw his cracks, his breaking point, and perhaps what humbled him for *South Pacific*—came during his short-lived stint on *Heroes vs. Villains.* After Sandra called him out at a Tribal Council for delegating but not pulling his weight on chores, he broke down back at camp.

"What did I do to deserve Sandra saying that tonight?" he asked Tyson, his ally from *Tocantins.* "There's never been someone like me out here and there's never going to be someone like me again. I did noble things out here and I look ignoble." He continued on an expletive laden rant about how he's "the man" and the only person who "won't fucking compromise." Then he began to cry. "Why doesn't anybody ever say anything good about me? Am I that bad of a person, man? I only act tough, but I'm sensitive." It was a moment we could see the weight of being this larger-than-life character come through. It's hard to be the joke.

"Just tell me how I can help," Tyson responded, giving the teary-eyed warrior a hug. "If you want me to coach you through it, I may tell you things you don't like, but it's going to turn out better for you. I promise you." "Like what?" Coach asked, stepping out of the hug, seemingly shocked there could be any criticism. Tyson responded honestly: "Don't wear feathers in your hair at Tribal. Don't tell your stories. People don't believe your stories, they mock you, there's no reason to tell them. Do your Tai Chi in private where nobody can see you."

X

"IN MY BRAIN, I had to find a balance between satisfying the audience and giving off the perception I want to have for myself. I want to be caring and respond to him accordingly, but I also don't wanna get looped into the ridiculousness of the things he's saying. I can't be so sympathetic that people are like, 'Oh, Tyson's wacky too,'" **Tyson Apostol** says, reflecting back on this moment over fifteen years later. His solution was just to be as honest as possible.

Tyson is another big *Survivor* personality—he's sassy and dry and whimsical. He's a different kind of outrageous than Coach, a more self-aware kind, but he's still over-the-top. "Coach and I were kind of the first of our archetype," Tyson says of the exaggerated character on *Survivor*. And the season they were both first on, *Tocantins*, was "the swing and the risk," to see if these over-the-top characters would resonate with viewers. "Before that it was like, let's get salt of the earth, real Americans that people can understand, or just hot people from LA. Those were the two options. And when they got Coach and I, there was a different kind of push," Tyson says.

Tyson and Coach threw the concepts of known archetypes out of the window. They weren't there to fit a mold, they were just weirdos, seemingly more aware of the performative aspect of the show.

Unlike Coach, who was often the butt of the joke, Tyson was in on the joke. He understands the absurdity of *Survivor*—a televised reality show where you're trying to survive on an island and brutally eliminate fellow players for a chance at a million dollars—and that he was there to have fun, to make people laugh.

TYSON WAS RAISED in a Mormon family in Utah. He's tall, with long blonde hair. He's lean, wiry, athletic. He grew up racing mountain bikes and was a top junior racer. Also a gifted swimmer, Tyson attended Brigham Young University on a swim scholarship. During college, he went to the Philippines for his two-year Mormon mission, but upon returning, he learned his swim scholarship had been cancelled. Without it, he dropped out of college, knowing, "school was just trying to trick me into getting a career after anyway."

I ask Tyson about his current relationship to the church. "Indifference on the side of, it's probably not true, but if I get to heaven and it is, I'll high-five Jesus for what a hilarious joke it was." Still, he sees how his mission could have helped his *Survivor* game. "I think dealing with different personalities and being able to communicate with strangers is a big benefit. Like, knocking on a door and selling people on the story of Jesus Christ being factual definitely will give you some skills."

After leaving BYU, Tyson returned to cycling, this time road racing, " 'cause if you want to get paid to ride a bike, you need to be on the road." He biked professionally in Switzerland and Belgium for seven years.

When Tyson returned to Utah, unsure of what was next, his dad encouraged him to apply for *Survivor.* He was competitive, athletic, smart; it made sense. Tyson had never watched the show, but his parents were big fans, the type of fans who, among a pool of friends, would make sure they were always recording on VHS in case someone missed an episode. Tyson was skeptical. "Nobody gets on these shows. This is so stupid, what a waste of time." He wrote a "pretty asinine" application about "how much ass I kick and how I deserve a million dollars" just to "prove to my dad that no one gets on these shows." He says ten minutes after he submitted, he got a call from a Los Angeles number on his Motorola Razr flip phone. "I'm going to ruin my dad's favorite show."

Casting director Lynne Spillman remembers his application: "kind of smart ass, really funny." She adds, "I don't remember Tyson being easy," putting it kindly. Tyson didn't read any of the rules when making his audition video. "It was like no background music. Mine had background music. No other people. Mine had a bunch of other people in it. Under three minutes. Mine was over three minutes," he says. But this refusal to comply with convention is exactly what makes him such a star.[23] Tyson was there to be "young and arrogant." Producers originally wondered if he was a Jonny Fairplay-type, but Tyson didn't have that heartlessness—he was his own thing.

When Tyson got to the Santa Monica hotel for interviews, he understood his job was to make waves, to be talked about. "I was born to push buttons," Tyson says.

He would take bites out of pastries on the breakfast buffet and then place them back on their stand, making sure people were watching. At the pool, he lathered himself with baby oil and wore a white speedo—"I think it was kind of see-through when it would get wet"—often lounging poolside, far longer than the allotted hour. Staying on a lower level at the hotel, he would get out of the elevators at his floor, reach his hand back in and hit every other number, before flipping everyone else off and turning away. Casting later told him multiple people threatened violence against him during their interviews. "Like, all these alpha bro dudes were so bugged at me," he says. "None of them got cast."

Like Richard Hatch, once Apostol got to Brazil, he knew to turn down the character he played during casting. He also says he didn't expect the deep bonds you make in this "ridiculous circumstance." "You go in with the idea of just betraying everyone and slitting everyone's throat, and then you get out there and you're like, oh, these guys are actually pretty cool."

Tyson connected with Coach early on, partly because Coach's voice reminded him of a kind Scout leader he'd known as a kid. "Then when he started sinking into his Dragon Slayer-Coach mode, it was totally different. It took me by surprise, but also I was in too deep with him at that point. And I still loved him."

In *Tocantins*, Tyson was the jester. He would get naked and do

23. Tyson also remembers being told that Executive Producer Mark Burnett's son particularly liked his audition video. After the initial broad reach of the early seasons, the remaining viewership was getting older, like Tyson's parents, and casting Tyson was part of a push to bring in younger viewers.

silly dances, and he was always quick with a sassy quip. He plays with this unique quality—a lightness, and understanding that it's just a game, coupled with a fierce competitiveness. It may just be a game, but he wants to win. As he explained in an early confessional: "Having somebody that can make you laugh in an environment like this where everybody is dirty and tired, I think people appreciate that. But, when it comes down to it I want that million dollars—a lot of expensive furs on my shoulders, jewels on my pretty fingers, I'm talking big time. I'll wear a tiara. A man tiara. Do they make those?"

Tyson measured his performance's success in laughter (and disruption). "If I could do something funny enough in an interview where they had to take a pause 'cause the camera guy was shaking from laughter, then I knew that I'd done it." He was aware, "It's an experience that not everybody gets to have. You can't fully control if you're gonna win, so you may as well have fun." He adds: "If I'm enjoying, even at someone else's expense, then I at least got that from it. Preferably at someone else's expense, someone I don't like."

On *Tocantins,* that "someone he didn't like" came in the form of the often-pouty model Sierra Reed. "Everyone was getting rubbed the wrong way by her . . . and I was like I'm going to step in and be the hero and spokesperson for the tribe," Tyson says. This came in the form of brutally cutting, albeit hilarious, reads. "I've never liked Sierra. To me she's of no worth. I mean, her parents probably love her. I can't imagine her boyfriend's that cool," he told the cameras. "I have no clue why she's out here, other than to just give hope to stupid people around the world."

After Sierra's closest ally, Brendan Synnott—the strongest of foes and the dragon whose slaying birthed the Dragon Slayer—was blindsided, Apostol was thrilled that Sierra would be cut next: "Tonight's Tribal Council is going to be awesome! I'm hoping Sierra will cry a lot . . . It's funny when people cry," he said, confident she'd be gone.

Ultimately, that night, there were no tears. It wasn't the "awesome" Tribal Tyson expected—this time, the joke was on him. Since he had already won several Immunity Challenges, but wasn't safe that day, his tribe decided it would be their best chance to take him out. Tyson was blindsided, getting eighth place. In his exit interview, he explained: "It's a little weird being outfoxed by an idiot, but I'm not crying over it." Sometimes, the jester also becomes the fool.

Tyson returned the following year for *Heroes vs. Villains*, where he faced another ironic and self-inflicted departure. Early on the Villains tribe, Tyson was part of that solid majority alliance, and they were set on eliminating Parvati Shallow or Russell Hantz. As we see it on the show, Boston Rob brings together this group of six—Tyson, Sandra, Courtney, Coach, and Jerri—with a plan to split the vote, putting three on each target. If either Parvati or Russell were hiding a secret Immunity Idol, they'd be forced to play it, leaving the other still with three votes. ("three and three," Cao Boi's [page 79] Plan Voodoo in action).

Tyson says splitting the vote was actually his idea. "I went to [Rob] to split the vote and he said no . . . And then came back and said, 'This is what we should do.' And I said, 'I already said that.' He was like, 'I know, but I wasn't really calculating it. Now it does make sense.'" We didn't see Tyson's initial conversation in the ultimate cut, just Rob organizing the strategy. (A theme, perhaps.)

Tyson wanted to prioritize getting Parvati out, threat that she was, but Rob was adamant that Tyson's vote go to Russell, "for the blowback that was coming." But Tyson wanted to make a splash even production wasn't expecting. In the long hours before Tribal Council, with little to do but think, he talked himself into switching his vote to Parvati, "to take control of what I want to happen." The move collapsed the split vote: Russell played an idol saving Parvati, and Tyson was sent home, 3-2, having received the votes of Russell, Parvati, and Danielle. Once again, Tyson flew too close to the sun.

After *Heroes vs. Villains*, Tyson figured his *Survivor* career was over. He went through casting for a few other seasons but got tired of "being dragged through the shit," of the extensive and unclear process. But ahead of the twenty-seventh season, Tyson was asked if his wife, Rachel, had any interest in playing on *Blood vs. Water*. She did. Airing in 2013, this season featured returning players playing with loved ones. (This is the season Rupert Boneham bowed out of for his wife, Laura, and in which Tina Wesson, playing with her daughter, returned through the Redemption duels.) It also took place in the same part of the Philippines Tyson had traveled so many years ago for his Mormon mission.

Tyson says he entered this game thinking that "people as talented as me don't win this game. They never have, they never will. So I'm just gonna go have fun and go as long as I can, but make sure that I'm having fun." He miscalculated again, but that was a good thing this time. Tyson ended up winning. Rachel was eliminated before the merge, so he brought together an alliance of the other "single" players, and picked the couples off. In the finale, he won in a 7-1-0 vote.

This win allowed Tyson to return a fourth time for Season 40, *Winners at War*. He was voted out early, but won his way back on an Edge of Extinction challenge that allowed an eliminated player to return at the merge. He was booted again, but believes he was "six inches away," from winning it all when he barely lost (to Natalie Anderson, page 170) in the second chance to return, when only five contestants remained.

THE "JACKASS" AND the "smart ass"—Coach and Tyson ushered in the era of big, brash characters on *Survivor* that didn't play into archetypes—or even subvert them. They proved that being a memorable character could be just as valuable—at least for engaging TV—as being a strong strategist. "You just need two to five wackadoos and the season's gonna be fine," Tyson says. "Coach and I were kind of the first ones in that realm." *Survivor*'s casting team has continued to seek out big personalities and cast the "wackadoos."[24]

Coach became the torchbearer for the seemingly delusional, larger-than-life characters you "love to hate, or hate to love, or hate to hate" (as he described himself in a strikingly introspective moment at the end of *Heroes vs. Villains*).

Tyson, by contrast, was laughing with the audience. His persona was built on the understanding that *Survivor* is a difficult game, but ultimately made to entertain. "It's not so much, 'What does the audience want?'" Tyson explains. "It's more like, what do I want the audience's perception of me to be?" He was never precious about how he presented himself, but in certain moments—like when his middle-aged friend who considers himself a noble warrior was breaking down in front of both him and the cameras—he considered, "How do I not come off as a total dick, but also not just totally lip service Coach . . . how do I approach this where Coach is getting what he needs from me, but the audience is also?"

This understanding has made him an indispensable character, both on *Survivor* and in the larger reality television universe. He helmed a new possibility: the career reality star. "One of my strongest attributes is my personality, and being able to articulate my thoughts," he tells me. As someone who didn't want to be "tricked" into a "real career," he figured, "I'm going to try to squeeze as much juice as I can out of this until it disappears." That juice hasn't run out. On top of four *Survivor* seasons, Tyson has appeared on *Marriage Boot Camp*, *The Challenge,* and *House of Villains*. His influence doesn't stop there: He cohosts The Ringer's *Survivor* podcast *The Pod Has Spoken*, and keeps tens of thousands of followers entertained on social media.

In the decade that passed between Tyson's *Survivor* debut in 2009

24. In fact, the casting choices made for the landmark Season 50, which includes Coach, seem to reflect a doubling down on this.

and most recent appearance in 2020, online platforms became a central force in society. Everyone is, in some way, performing for the camera. The performance of self that Apostol understood on the show has become a constant in our everyday lives.

This shift in public understanding has also helped larger swaths of audiences embrace campy players like Coach and Tyson, much like Parvati's newfound belovedness. With streaming more accessible than ever and performance ubiquitous, Tyson has seen viewers embrace the wacky character—an understanding of performance. He says, "People now are able to recognize that and celebrate that," in a way they hadn't when he first played.

This is especially true for his dear friend, the Dragon Slayer. During *Tocantins*, Tyson saw that most viewers "really hated Coach—unless you were celebrating the truly absurd." It's part of what added to the pain Coach felt during that late-night breakdown. But today, Coach is celebrated. "People look back at *Tocantins* and are like, 'Coach is hilarious, he's so awesome, he's our favorite.'"

"Unbreakable, unbending, unmoving, immeasurable, immovable, invincible." Of course, dear reader, the path of the noble warrior is seldom straight, never simple. Yet through hurricanes, and Amazonian capture, through the jeers of nonbelievers and the woes of misgivings, the Dragon Slayer endures. What once seemed delusion has, over time, been transfigured into legend. The dragons have been slayed.

J.T. Thomas

J.T. THOMAS—WHO YOU MAY REMEMBER FROM "STUPIDEST move in *Survivor* history" fame for giving his idol to Russell Hantz (page 97)—first appeared in *Tocantins* alongside Coach and Tyson, where he played a not-stupid game. While he wasn't the same over-the-top player as his *Tocantins* castmates, it was his own "character" and understanding of that perception that ultimately helped him win that season.

J.T. Thomas, a soft-spoken twenty-four-year old cattle rancher from Alabama, knew how to play up that good-old-boy Southern charm perfectly. Upon first seeing Thomas, his quick-witted tribemate, Stephen Fishbach, fretted: "When I see there's at least one good old fashion Southern boy here I'm concerned. I don't see him loving the anxious New York Jew." But just as quickly, Fishbach's tune changed: "He might just be seducing me with his pretty country ways, but I'm smitten." Stephen and J.T. would become best friends—a duo rivaled only by the now-married Rob and Amber—and go to the end together. The neurotic strategist and the beloved gentleman made for a formidable pair.

But it wasn't just Stephen—J.T. charmed the pants off of everyone with his Southern gentility. He easily became the leader of his tribe, a charismatic presence who put other players at ease and earned their loyalty almost effortlessly.[25] Entering the merge down in num-

25. In a rare moment in *Survivor* history, Brendan Synnott (Coach's "dragon"), tells the camera in a confessional: "If I take J.T. in the finals with me, he's gonna

bers, he was quickly embraced by Coach for the "honor and integrity" he displayed. He joined Coach's Power Alliance, where he was dubbed "The Warrior," (Stephen was "The Wizard," and Tyson, the "Assistant Coach"). During Touchy Subjects—a challenge in which players answer revealing questions about one another—J.T. was unanimously chosen as the castaway they'd trust with their lives. He later told cameras: "I don't know why everyone trusts me so much. In this game, I'm not so trustworthy, and it seems like people don't catch on to that. It may be the accent, I don't know." This would foreshadow another unanimous vote that was coming his way.

J.T.'s magnetism and some "not so trustworthy" moves got him to the end, where he once again charmed the jury as he made his case for the million, emphasizing that he brought his loyal ally, Stephen, over someone who may have been easier to beat. Ultimately, it didn't matter who J.T. brought, because he won unanimously. J.T. played *Survivor*'s first "perfect game"—an impressive feat where you don't receive a single vote for elimination during the game, and then receive every jury votes to win. That season, he also won the fan favorite prize.

---

beat me. I know it's crazy, but for me, winning in this game is about getting to an outcome at the end of the game which is going to satisfy me. If he wins it, that's like me winning this game."

John Cochran

SURVIVOR'S SECOND—AND THUS FAR ONLY OTHER—PERFECT game came from a very different player.

In this *game of society*, casting had found the jocks, the mean girls, and the wacky uncles in the All-American Heroes, Black Widows, and Dragon Slayers. But there was one archetype *Survivor* hadn't yet mastered: the nerd. There had been plenty of smart, calculated players, but to be able to survive the grueling conditions on the show, they rarely looked the type—if hunky Yul Kwon was supposed to be a nerd, *Survivor* clearly had a long way to go.

Production's prayers were finally answered in the form of a super nerd: **John Cochran**. He wasn't just a nerd, but a nerd about *Survivor*. He had grown up as one of the show's biggest fans. He was a Columbia-educated Harvard Law student who had written an award-winning paper about *Survivor*. And importantly, he looked the part: pale white skin, square glasses, and scrawny arms that didn't show off the hundred pushups he had trained himself to do before filming. If *Survivor* was going to perfect the nerd, they were going to go all out. "This is not a guy who should be on this show. His skin has never seen the sun, he doesn't know how to find food or fish, he's afraid of the water," Jeff described in a pre-show interview. It seemed almost cruel to put him on a remote island in this demanding game, but it was there that he found himself, and there that he would shape a story that helped make him legend.

—————

AFTER HEARING ADS for this wild new show—"it sounded like people were going to die on the island"—a thirteen-year-old John Cochran, living in the Washington, DC, suburbs, was one of the curious millions who tuned in for that first episode of *Survivor*. "What even is this genre of television?" he thought at the time. "I always used to be big into old game shows, and my favorite part of the game show is seeing people that ordinarily wouldn't be on TV. Suddenly they're on a TV set and Alex Trebek is asking them little personal questions . . . you get insight into these people," John says. "Suddenly *Survivor* arrives and it's like that little element of game shows, but magnified times a thousand."

The story of John's love of *Survivor* runs parallel to the wider audience's relationship to the show. It began with curiosity and became infatuation: "What the hell is this?" became "This is the coolest thing in the world!" For the first couple seasons, John says every student and teacher at school was watching and discussing *Survivor*. After that novelty wore off for his classmates, the excited post-episode chatter whittled down to just him and the secretary at the principal's office, "so I would go check in with her every week after the episode aired."

Season after season, John's passion for this experiment endured. In high school, *Survivor* was his identity. He wrote newsletters about the show and handed them out, he wore *Survivor* buffs every day, and at study hall, he would draw the logo from "loving memory" in his notebooks. "It should have been the source of bullying, but somehow I avoided that," he says.

By college, he felt like "a loner in my passion." He tried to proselytize the good word of *Survivor*, but it didn't stick. Still, he watched religiously—alone. At Harvard, he wrote a paper for a class on what the judicial system could learn from *Survivor*'s jury system, which won him a Dean's Prize. (John insists it was a minor paper, but an award-winning Harvard Law School paper on the game of

Survivor became a major selling point for casting and later production while introducing this super nerd to audiences; it is the topic of his very first confessional, within the first two minutes of the season's first episode).

Despite his deep love for the show, John hadn't seriously considered applying. He thought: "It just seems like reality TV is meant for a different personality type—a bit more adventurous and outgoing and outdoorsy and social and strong and stuff." That all changed when he met none other than Yul Kwon.

John was interning at the FCC during law school—proselytizing the show, as usual—when some interns in another bureau mentioned their supervisor had been on *Survivor*. "It was freaking Yul Kwon!" They offered to introduce John, but "I'm not gonna freaking meet him right now. What are you talking about?" He needed a few days to prepare. Yul remembers his interns telling him about John. "Oh cool, have him come by." His intern informed him John wasn't ready. "What do you mean he's not ready?" Eventually the fateful meeting happened. John saw Yul was "a normal, well-adjusted guy that's also ambitious and successful and it didn't ruin his life." As Yul remembers, "he was like a total nerd about it."

John applied to *Survivor*, emphasizing his lifelong dedication to the show. He ended his video saying, "Or you can cast me for no other reason than to destroy the promising legal career of a Harvard Law student." Throughout the interview process, John played up the super nerd. He looked the part and his fandom came naturally. He remembers looking around the Santa Monica hotel where the interviews took place. He saw "the hunky beach studs and the athletes and there are the military guys and there are the bikini babes," but nowhere did he see some version of himself. He had no competition for his type: "I feel like if I went on the show now it would be harder for me 'cause there's a lot of overeducated anxious nerds who love *Survivor* that go on the show." John originated this archetype, and it stuck.

Wardrobe leaned into it too, putting him in a pink button down shirt and a red sweater vest. "I've never worn a sweater vest in my life. Also, I have rosacea and blotchy skin. I don't wanna wear bright pink and bright red clothes." But the wardrobe staff knew how to make the argument: "She said, 'You know, there are certain wardrobe items, there's a tie dye shirt, there's a Boston Red Sox cap, and now there's gonna be a red sweater vest,'" Cochran recalls. The idea of being up there with legends like Rupert Boneham and Boston Rob certainly helped convince him, and it became true: the red sweater vest lives among the most iconic looks in *Survivor*'s clothing history.

John Cochran was cast for *South Pacific,* that 2011 season that saw Coach and Ozzy return as "captains." And he seemed eager to become part of the history of the show he had long loved. In the opening moments, as Jeff Probst "meets" the players, he calls on John: "Guy in the back, what's your name?" "John," John answered, then continued, "Well, okay. I know the players you really like, you tend to call by their last name, so I was hoping you could call me Cochran. Continuing the tradition of [Colby] Donaldson, [Johnathan] Penner, [Rob] Mariano. Cochran, I think I fit in that lineage perfectly," John said. "All great players, we'll see if you live up, Cochran," Jeff responded seriously.

For John, this was all a bit tongue-and-cheek. "Jeff only likes these alpha guys. The only people he roots for are like Colby the Cowboy . . . these Captain America looking guys like [Andrew] Savage or Hunter Ellis. So for me it was kind of poking fun at that. 'Sorry I'm not one of your boy toys, Jeff, but you're going to learn to love me instead.'" John embraced the campiness of it all, and with that embrace he did something else: he changed the face of who those players Jeff loves are, he expanded who got to belong in that lineage. John taught *Survivor* to love the nerd.

Behind the scenes, the interaction was a bit more produced than it appeared. John had casually mentioned this last name idea to Jeff during casting, and they ate it up. In that island opening, after simply answering his name was, "John," Jeff followed up: "And do you want to go by John?" That part was cut in post, but John decided to play along. "That's when I was like, you know what, I'm gonna lean into this thing. That was my first little test of whether I'm gonna embrace the whole situation." Leaning in paid off. John become a darling of production. The different names gave him a degree of "personality compartmentalization." With that, Cochran was born.

This marked the start of a symbiotic relationship between production and Cochran as a character. Production got to show off this persona incarnate of *Survivor*'s cultural importance, wrapped in the package of a nerd who gave it intellectual legitimacy. As Cochran, John got to brand this new archetype on a show he deeply loved. The personality compartmentalization had its limits. At his core, Cochran was still John and vice versa. The show breaks you down quickly and "schticks aren't sustainable." But in interviews with producers for the confessionals, Cochran was "clocking in to do a job," looking to satisfy—a self-awareness not unlike Tyson's. As a superfan, John knew when to turn on his performance and understood what made for great commentary.

In casting this super nerd, *Survivor* was doing more than fulfilling an archetype—they were experimenting with a new role for production: the narrator. John is smart and funny, he's self-deprecating and knows how to tell a good story—even more, he understands the game inside and out. He provided ideal color commentary and became a great narrator for this season. He got lots of screen time with his witty confessionals, becoming a central character on *South Pacific*. But in the game itself, Cochran found himself on the outs.

He was on what he called the "*90210* Tribe," led by Ozzy and mostly filled with young, hot, athletic people. In their first moments at camp, rather than starting on shelter, Ozzy told everyone to take off their clothes and take a swim in their underwear. These returning captains set a tone, a value system of the tribe. And with Ozzy that was: "Are you a young, attractive person I am either into, or will be good at challenges?" John says. "I was neither of those, so from the beginning I felt insecure." Perhaps fitting for the nerd archetype, Cochran was outside of the "cool alliance" that ran his tribe.

He received elimination votes at seven different Tribal Councils, a record he still holds, but somehow avoided being voted out before the merge. Still, "being the other option every episode is a horrible feeling," he says.

At the merge, both tribes entered with equal numbers, but Cochran flipped, giving the numbers to Coach's alliance. In hindsight, he says, "I was joining a group of people that were in a crazy cult that were all, like, maniacs," but "anybody in my position with a modicum of self-respect, wouldn't stick with the group telling you they were trying to vote you off." This gave Coach's alliance the advantage in numbers to Pagong Ozzy's Savaii Tribe, but once the Savaii were all gone, Cochran was next.

JOHN HAD EAGERLY watched every episode of *Survivor* before, but despite his superfandom, watching his own season back was "very unpleasant." Being typecast as the nerd can be tricky. "They chose lots of embarrassing stuff, or decontextualized things I was saying. It was leaning into me being really awkward." He says the day after episodes aired was the worst, "'cause you're up all night just reading every single comment." During this 2011 season, those comments were mostly on the message boards or comment sections of websites, but by his next game, airing just two years later, commentary on social media sites like Twitter and Reddit had taken off.

Still, when *Survivor* called back just a month after his first season had stopped airing to see if Cochran wanted to play again, he was in. He wasn't eager about his options at law school, plus "it's a flattering thing that this show you've been obsessed with for a long time is like, 'we're calling you back 'cause we like you so much and we wanna see you again right away.'"

The twenty-sixth season, *Survivor: Caramoan*, which aired in 2013, was another take on the *Fans vs. Favorites* concept from *Micronesia*, though casting seemed to very loosely interpret the term "favorites." Cochran mostly fit the bill (he was a competitor for the fan favorite vote on his first season but ultimately lost to Ozzy). There were squeals of excitement when he hopped out of the chopper, though someone also shouted, "nerd alert!"

The others in his group were a far cry from the *90210* tribe of his previous season. It included Phillip Sheppard, a branch off the Coach tree of delusion, who claimed to be a former Special Agent, and played the game in hot pink panties; and Brandon Hantz, the even less-stable nephew of Russell Hantz, who had to leave the game after dumping the tribe's rice out and threatening violence against Sheppard. Even poor gaslit Erik Reichenbach, the Brigade-befuddled ice cream scooper from the first *Fans vs. Favorites*, was back. Cochran was still the nerd, but among this group, he was the cool, "normal" one—or at least one of the more emotionally-regulated ones. This season seemed to be an over-correction of that "wackadoo" casting Tyson and Coach once pioneered.

Cochran entered this season ready to win. His deadened self-consciousness meant he was almost confident: "Your self-esteem and pride gets so punctured by being on the show that the second time you're just like, whatever." He had clarity in his goal. He had the experience of being a big character, "which was neat but not that enjoyable for me." This time, he was expressly there to win. Maybe this time there was more of John the person in Cochran the player.

This confidence and clarity became a lethal combo. Cochran wasn't just the show's central narrator—though he was still great at that—he was its central player. He was in the thick of it, strategically and socially. Not necessarily a defining force, but a vital one. "My opinion was valued and I'd hear out other people," he says. The nerd who was on the outs of his first tribe for his lack of challenge ability won three challenges in this follow-up season. "The guy that got screamed at for not unclipping a thing on his first challenges now won more immunities than anyone. Even if they were goofy immu-nities, everyone had the same opportunity to win them," he says.

Cochran practically sailed to the finale, winning challenges and never receiving any votes. At Final Tribal, he put his great oratory skills to work and presented a compelling case for himself. "This is the culmination of thirteen years of passion for *Survivor*," he told the jury. "I know I can't out-muscle, I know I can't out-charm, I don't even think I can really out-strategize anybody, but I can beat people in timing." He took the threats out before they could get to him.

Almost a year later, at the live reunion, this super nerd received unanimous votes awarding him the win, playing the show's second ever "perfect" game.

"I don't think I could have done much better than I did out there, which is like—usually I beat myself up over everything," the ever-diffident John says about his performance at Final Tribal. But that self-awareness made him more attuned to how the same game played out differently for his closest ally. He calls out the treatment Utah mother of six Dawn Meehan received from the jury.[26] He feels he and Dawn played similar games as close allies, and sees how "ageism and sexism" means older women are often cast into maternal roles. "Even if they're not acting like a mom, the other contestants are like, 'you're the mom of the tribe.' And then that creates this emotional dynamic that when, when that person votes you off. You're like, 'Screw you. You're my mom out here. How could you do that to me.'" Unlike the mom, the nerd didn't have the same expectations of fealty and care placed on them.

Still, John's understanding of the social dynamics that may have shaped the vote does nothing to take away from his impressive, "perfect," win. In fact, like J.T. before, it was this understanding of his archetype and conscious choice to play into how he was cast that helped elevate him to win the game. He won by reading the room. He knew the story he was telling.

26. In one of the more haunting moments on *Survivor*, an angered juror, Brenda Lowe, asked Dawn to take out her false teeth in an effort to humiliate her. Meehan had lost them in the water during the game, a major insecurity for her, and even considered quitting, but Brenda had helped her find them. Dawn submitted, taking out her teeth and revealing her toothless bottom lip, but she still didn't receive Brenda's vote.

Cochran has been asked to return to *Survivor* again, many times, and asked onto other shows in the genre, but he's not interested. He feels like the seasons he played blurred together into "a three-year cycle." He hated the experience of having to watch himself, even while playing a "perfect" game. "Being on TV is not fun for me," he's learned.

He also recognizes Cochran's story has been told, perfectly: The kid who had long loved *Survivor* played the game, once as the nerdy outcast, but came back to win it all. "I was a thirteen-year-old kid that was obsessed with this show for such a long time. And then, not only do I get to play, I get to come back and I win and I get every vote," John says. "The second time felt like I was writing a love letter to *Survivor*. It was like writing a fanfic, like "Oh, I'm winning challenges now, and I'm in an alliance, and I'm getting votes to win.'"

The *Survivor* finale announcing his perfect win came one week before he graduated from law school. But John never pursued law. With his wit and knack for storytelling, Jeff encouraged him to pursue television writing and helped him make connections to get a job in the industry. It was a well-deserved next step for John—though certainly vastly different treatment than the career hindrance someone like Sean Rector faced.

Cochran wasn't the first nerd to play the game. There were plenty of smart and spectacled players before him. He wasn't the first *Survivor* superfan to play either.[27] But John was the first to tell that story, to put it all together. He told the epic tale of outcast-turned-victor and in doing so, incarnated the archetype and proved it as a way to win—rather than reject or subvert, he embraced his role, and shaped it. John showed how these smart, funny players who know the show well can bring a new level of commentary to the game. Soon, super nerds would become fixtures of *Survivor*.

27. Sherri Biethman, a finalist in Cochran's winning game, was also a super fan and had named her son Colby after Donaldson, part of that 166 percent jump in the name's popularity after his debut on *Survivor*.

Kelley Wentworth
& Rob Cesternino

FOR THE CASUAL VIEWER, COCHRAN MIGHT HAVE BEEN THE FIRST proof of the depth and ferocity of the *Survivor* fandom—that after more than a decade, there were many who knew the game inside and out. But behind the scenes, the number of superfans was already vast and growing, and an ever-expanding media landscape was creating opportunities for these fans to interact with each other and players alike.

Kelley Wentworth was a fan from the very beginning: She started watching *Survivor*'s first season with her dad, Dale, in their eastern Washington farming town when she was just a teenager. She was instantly captivated. For a while, it was a passion shared mainly with her dad. Soon, though, she would learn about the big world of message boards and podcasts and social media conversations, and become an active member in the online *Survivor* fandom.

Kelley and Dale wanted to compete on a game show together. They originally applied to CBS's *The Amazing Race* as a father-daughter duo. But Lynne Spillman, who cast both—and who Kelley calls "one of the greatest casting people that has ever been in the business"—reached out about another option: *Survivor* was bringing back the *Blood vs. Water* theme—playing with a loved one, like Tyson's winning game—but this time with all new players.

Kelley and Dale were cast for the 2014 *Survivor: San Juan del Sur* as "the farmer and the farmer's daughter." It was a dream come true, but a short run. Kelley's reputation as a fan made her look dangerous; a tribe swap left her on the wrong side of numbers, and she left in Episode 5. Dale followed immediately after.

"Oh, I was devastated," Kelley says. "I kind of had just started to get into the rhythm of how the show worked and how to play the game. And then I was gone." She had shown some sass and sparkle on the show she had loved for so long, but among the hundreds who had played the game, this early boot didn't make a splash.

Kelley heard word of a returning player season coming up—these "spread like wildfire" among former players—but she didn't think there was a chance that she would get a call based on her performance in San Juan del Sur.

To her surprise, she did. "I had one producer that really went to bat for me," she says. "She says she saw a lot of potential in me . . . she saw how much I wanted to play." But with this particular upcoming season, wanting to play, even wooing casting, wouldn't be enough.

AT THIS POINT, the twenty-teens, a growing social media landscape changed the shape of how to watch *Survivor*. A few seasons earlier, the show introduced hashtags at certain key moments—#blindside, #idol, #GastrointestinalDistress—to get online conversation churning. Jeff Probst would live-Tweet during episodes.

Survivor: Cambodia, the 2015 season, would be the ultimate test case of fan interactivity. The theme was "Second Chance," allowing former players who had never won a chance to return. Production contacted seventy-five players and whittled it down to a list of thirty-two, but then the power shifted. The ultimate cast (ten men and ten women) would come down to an online fan vote.

Kelley had miraculously made it onto the ballot. Now she had an uphill battle—casual viewers might not remember an early boot from a couple seasons back. But to her advantage, superfans probably would remember this fellow superfan, a player who was an eager and active part of their community. These kinds of online fans, while a small portion of the audience, were also the ones who would be religiously voting, and they congregated where Kelley already lived—on *Survivor* Twitter, Reddit, and podcasts.

Kelley wanted back bad, and she began a hardcore campaign. "It was like a full-time job," she says. She made videos for YouTube, she did AMAs on Reddit and made countless Twitter posts with #VoteWentworth.[28] For his part, Dale posted flyers around their Washington town. Kelley also appeared on podcasts, and importantly, she was already known to the fans of one particular podcast, which held a lot of sway in this fan ecosystem.

BEFORE HE BUILT a media empire, **Rob Cesternino** helped change how *Survivor* was played. Playing on *Survivor: Amazon*, the sixth season in 2003, he was among the early developers of strategy. He had watched every episode of the thus far short-lived game and knew it well; he was the first "Know-It-All" character type. He brought a uniquely flexible approach to alliances—pioneering "flip-flopping," the term that would come to describe players fluidly turning on alliances at whim to change the numbers. He was taken out at the final three by the eventual winner, Jenna Morasca, as a threat to win (this is when Final Tribal was only two). Then, he returned for *All-Stars* but was an early target, the third player eliminated. Jeff called him "the smartest player to never win."

After playing twice in close succession, Cesternino wasn't sure what was next for him. Early in life, game shows were his biggest passion, he wanted to be a game show host. He went to school to study broadcasting, and then landed on *Survivor*—after initially interviewing for *Big Brother*. Now that he had had "the most fun that I had ever had in my life"—what could he do next?

Rob moved to L.A. to work for "The Fishbowl," a short-lived website that was an early attempt at digital content for former reality TV stars. The career options were not nearly as established as they

28. Kelley Wentworth was using her last name, not for Cochran reasons, but because Kelly Wiglesworth, the "rat" runner up to Richard Hatch from Season 1, was also in the running.

are today (institutionalized in that career reality star era of Tyson and more) but there was a growing number of shows. Now beyond just *The Real World* and *Survivor*, there was *American Idol, The Bachelor, America's Next Top Model, Big Brother, The Amazing Race* and many more (often questionably executed) experiments within the genre. The Fishbowl had former contestants writing articles and hosting "internet radio shows." Even after the site failed, Rob continued working with producers to make content for YouTube and MySpace, before the 2008 recession left their funding dry.

Soon-to-be-married and unsure of what his career looked like next, Cesternino picked up a mic and started *Rob Has a Podcast* (RHAP) early in 2010.[29] It began as him and his now-wife Nicole, discussing the season airing at the time: the much-anticipated *Heroes vs. Villains*. A few episodes in, he started bringing on the greats as guests—Jonny Fairplay and Ethan Zohn, Yau-Man Chan and Richard Hatch. He found particular success with *Tocantins* runner-up Stephen Fishbach, a fellow "Know-It-All" who had never won. They began live recapping episodes as *The Survivor Know-It-Alls*. RHAP grew steadily, with eager fans excited to hear analysis of the episode they had just watched or get updates from former players they couldn't yet keep tabs on, especially in these early days of social media.

Today, RHAP is an empire of podcasts, with almost seventy listed on their site. They have won several awards for the thousands of hours of content produced. They have nearly 200,000 subscribers on YouTube, with videos regularly eclipsing 100,000 views. Many members pay for a Patreon that offers more interactivity and community. What ESPN did to sports and CNN did to news, RHAP did to *Survivor*—it provided a near-constant stream of content and analysis that allows for fandom to go far beyond the weekly episodes.

There are recaps and exit interviews and new shows and inside jokes—a shared language for the superfans. This level of analysis

29. Notably, this was four years before *Serial* was released and revolutionized the world of podcasts.

meant fans weren't just watching the show, but thinking deeply about strategy and production: Who got more airtime? How is their edit being portrayed? What historical foundation is this strategy building on? Viewers began thinking of *Survivor* in a meta way, and with players increasingly coming from the superfan base, this way of thinking made its way onto the island.

Alongside RHAP, an entire media network was growing around *Survivor*. Journalists like Dalton Ross and Mike Bloom have made the show their beat, and often appear as guests on RHAP. Countless other sites and podcasts have flourished—I often consulted the well-updated, fan-run SurvivorWiki in my research.

Kosta Psaltis was a "month one" listener of RHAP and *Survivor* superfan since he was a kid, starting with *All-Stars*. He is a "data-oriented person" and started tracking *Survivor* data like challenge winners and boot orders "as pure personal interest." Around 2011, when Jeff Probst started live-Tweeting *Survivor* episodes, Tyson Apostol joked on RHAP that the podcast recaps should be live-Tweeted too. Kosta took up the role, Tweeting and sharing kernels of the data he collected as @RobsFactChecker on Twitter. During *Winners at War*, with the encouragement of his now-wife, he began putting some more effort into his visuals, sharing not just screenshots of Excel sheets, but elegant charts and graphs to an audience of tens of thousands on Instagram. He has helped guide fact-based conversations about the show, referring to metrics on players' allotted screen time, or tracking player popularity through online follower growth.

If Kosta is *Survivor*'s analyst, Kris C. is its archivist. Kris has been a devoted fan since day one who always found time for

Survivor—even using VPNs and coordinating schedules around it to watch live from remote hostels while spending a year backpacking in Australia. In 2020, when Kris's niece told him that he was too old to be successful on social media, he took it as a challenge. He thought about what he knew best—*Survivor*—and started posting casting updates for *Winners at War* and clips from the show. "People gravitated toward it. It's not that I'm stuck doing this page, but I'm kind of a victim of my own success. It got bigger than I could have ever imagined," he says. Kris posts as @AllWinnersSurvivor to over 100,000 followers on Instagram and more across platforms. He uses his knack for finding "hidden tidbits," like historic videos, deleted scenes, and interview clips. (It was thanks to his post I found Sandra Diaz-Twine's audition tape, one she says she mailed to CBS and had never posted online.) Jeff Probst has even sent Kris a note, thanking him for how he has shaped the *Survivor* fandom on social media.

Unlike Kosta and Kris and so many others, I'm not an active superfan in the online *Survivor* community. I spoke to both Kosta and Kris as I researched for this book, and consulted the brilliant work of so many others who dedicate time adding to the *Survivor* ecosystem.

One of the early moments that proved RHAP could move audiences came from the Miss Survivor pageant. Looking for ways to entertain fans in the off-season between *Survivor* and *Big Brother*, Rob created his own (slightly dated) drama: Miss Survivor. The first competition in 2012 pit every former female player up against each other. Fans voted for a few finalists, who participated in interviews on RHAP, showing off a talent, and then in a debate. Fittingly, Parvati Shallow won this first Miss Survivor. In future years, the competition would only involve the women who had played in the two seasons that year. The competition garnered thousands of votes, with players getting involved with write-in campaigns and live-tweeting commentary. It proved that this *Survivor* fandom would show up and engage.

In what would end up being the last pageant, Miss Survivor 2015's finalists included the *San Juan del Sur* eventual winner, Natalie Anderson (page 170), *Survivor: Cagayan* sixth-place finisher and challenge dominator, Tasha Fox, and Kelley Wentworth as its finalists. As Rob and 2014 Miss Survivor Andrea Boehlke announced the finalists, they were surprised that Kelley had made it, but noted that she had been "playing the game," posing in her RHAP shirt, appearing in other podcasts in the RHAP universe—campaigning hard for this prize.

Kelley didn't become Miss Survivor—Natalie took the sash and tiara that year—but she had further ingratiated herself with the fans, and particularly the RHAP community. Just a few months later, she would be back on the show, campaigning for a much bigger prize: her second chance.

THE FINAL CAST for *Survivor: Cambodia—Second Chance* was announced at the live reunion of the previous season, *Survivor: One World*. The thirty-two finalists sat in groups in the audience, waiting in anticipation with their bags packed—they would be heading straight to film, but only twenty would make the cut. "I was planning two different lives," Kelley says. Her husband was in Miami for a wedding and she told him: "Well, I'll either see you at the wedding in a couple days or I'll be leaving." She had to plan work as if she would be away, but she knew there was a chance she was coming back. Even with her extensive campaigning and in with the fandom, Kelley was fighting an uphill battle against legends of the game.

The announcement began. "Tens of millions of votes cast," Jeff proclaimed. "Give us some music, David Vanacore," he added, shouting out the brilliant long-time composer of *Survivor,* who has underlined some of TV's most dramatic moments with musical flair. Suspenseful music began.

Jeff first walked up to the other Kelly—Kelly Wiglesworth. "Season 1—over 125 million unique individuals . . . watched this moment right here when Richard Hatch beat you by one vote . . . I'm so happy to say, Kelly Wiglesworth, you will get another shot! Get up on that stage!" She ran up, with a pump of the arm and a big smile. Jeff Varner, who got bested by Tina's smart strategizing at the merge in Season 2, was back. Terry Dietz from Cirie's first season was in too, but Shane Powers from the same season was not. Poor Teresa "T-Bird" Cooper, who back in *Africa* had warned her teammates of Ethan Zohn's likability, didn't make it (though she would later make up for it with her own show on the RHAP network, *Talking with T-Bird*).

Finally, Jeff came to Wentworth's row. "Alright, get this big shot, because we have four young, beautiful, smart strategists. One of the most lethal types of people to play this game," he said. "Two of you will get a shot, two of you will not." He announced Monica Padilla from *Survivor: Samoa* was in. "Kelley Wentworth," he said, then paused dramatically. "You will get a second chance!" Kelley jumped up to the sound of cheers and applause, grabbing her brown and pink duffle and running up on stage.

"It was such a weird feeling," Kelley says, about sitting up on that stage. "You're so excited. All this work and you're gonna go play on this epic season. And then you look out at the face of the T-Birds of the world and Shane and these people who have been wanting to play and you feel horrible at the same time."

Kelley's campaign had been successful. She had used the fandom to get herself back onto *Survivor.* She'd already been playing for months, but now the real game was starting. "We were full of joy, excitement, and then we had to go and immediately go on lockdown and couldn't talk to each other," she says. They got on an awaiting bus, and eventually made their way to Cambodia.

Despite successfully getting onto the show, Kelley was an underdog from the get-go. She had played the fewest days of any player on the cast. Many others had relationships (and pre-game alliances) from their more extended time in the *Survivor* player community. Kelley found herself on the outside of the majority for almost her entire time on the island. Still, she was determined to play a strong, strategic game. She wiggled her way out of sticky situations with nimble strategic moves: flipping with the numbers as needed, pitting allies against each other, using her idols effectively. At the merge, she had proven herself a strategic threat and was the clear target, but successfully played her idol to the shock of her tribe. "Wentworth, doesn't count," Jeff read, pulling out vote-after-vote against Kelley. She had successfully voided nine votes against her with an idol, a record that still stands. She continued to skillfully navigate the game, winning two Immunity Challenges and successfully playing a second idol to save herself (adding to the record books as the first person to successfully play multiple idols to save themselves in a single season). Eventually, at the final four, she was deemed far too big of a threat and eliminated just before Final Tribal Council. After the disappointment of her first season, Kelley had campaigned her way back into *Survivor*'s history books.

"Without the fans, I felt like I never would be here," Kelley says. "Without the fandom, without supporters, nobody gets to play the game. So it was important to me to give back in some way." Kelley has stayed active in the fandom. After her season, she set up a PO box and responded to every piece of fan mail she got. "I still have it all in my garage, it truly means so much to me," she says. Today, she has become a core part of that very media ecosystem that helped establish her in the *Survivor* universe. She entertains hundreds of thousands of TikTok followers with *Survivor* commentary, reenactments, and behind-the-scenes insight.

Kelley played once more, on the thirty-eighth season, *Edge of Extinction*, lasting into the merge. For now, though, she's enjoying life again as just a fan. "I have an opinion, just like you. I love the show, just like you. I'm mad at Jeff sometimes, just like you," she says. "Connecting with fellow fans is what makes the show great to begin with. That's why families get together on Wednesday nights and watch it. That's why we have [fantasy *Survivor*] drafts. That's why people go on podcasts and talk about it. That's why people are on social media the next day."

Kelley Wentworth got the boot at the final four when she returned in Cambodia. In the thirty-third season, *Millennials vs. Gen X*, it was the anxious TV writer-turned-dominant-force, David Wright (a super nerd of the Cochran mold) who faced the fourth-place torch snuff. In his return on *Survivor: Game Changers*, Season 34, the beloved Tai Trang, too, was booted just one spot from the finals. By its thirty-fifth season, *Survivor* announced a twist: Final Four Fire-Making. Essentially, the Immunity Challenge winner would choose which players would safely enter the finale, while the other two would fight for their spot with a fire-making challenge. Jeff Probst explained (on an official accompaniment podcast of his own, *On Fire with Jeff Probst*, which launched in 2023) that it was a "forgone conclusion" that the most popular, likable characters could rarely make it to the end—as big threats to win. The Final Four Fire-Making challenge guaranteed that players like Kelley, who had earned the audience's affection and played a strong game, could at least fight for a seat at the end. It's a twist that changed the dynamic of the game, with future players deciding who to put into the fire-making challenge, or even placing themselves at risk for a "resume move." And one that led to several edge-of-your-seat showdowns.

To Kelley, engaging with *Survivor* is about so much more than tuning in to your television one night a week: It's about sharing the experience of fandom and making human connections. Whether discussing the most loved and hated players, the best and worst strategic moves, or which grubs you would willingly eat in desperate times, the creation of the media ecosystem around *Survivor* allowed it to become about more than just the show. It became about the community.

(Left to right) Richard Hatch, Kelly Wiglesworth, and Rudy Boesch during the iconic Hands on a Hard Idol challenge, *Survivor: Borneo*. *CBS Photo Archive via Getty Images*

Richard Hatch as a child. *Courtesy of Richard Hatch*

Sandra Diaz-Twine (left) and Richard Hatch (right) connecting off the island. *Courtesy of Richard Hatch*

Sean Rector rep-
ping his "whole
New York vibe
look" on the streets
of New York City.
Courtesy of Sean Rector

Sean Rector (center) with
friends at his sixth grade
graduation in Harlem.
Courtesy of Sean Rector

Left: Colby Donaldson (left) and Tina Wesson (right) at a red carpet event after *Survivor: The Australian Outback*. *CBS Photo Archive via Getty Images*
Right: Boston Rob Mariano (left) and Amber Brkich (right) during *Survivor: All-Stars* where they fell in love. *CBS Photo Archive via Getty Images*

Jonny Fairplay (left) and Rupert Boneham (right) at a red carpet event after *Survivor: Pearl Island*.
CBS Photo Archive via Getty Images

(Left to right) Russell Hantz, Parvati Shallow, and Sandra Diaz-Twine at the finale of *Survivor: Heroes vs. Villains*. #QueenStaysQueen. *CBS Photo Archive via Getty Images*

The Dragon Slayer (Benjamin "Coach" Wade) practicing his secretive martial art. *CBS Photo Archive via Getty Images*

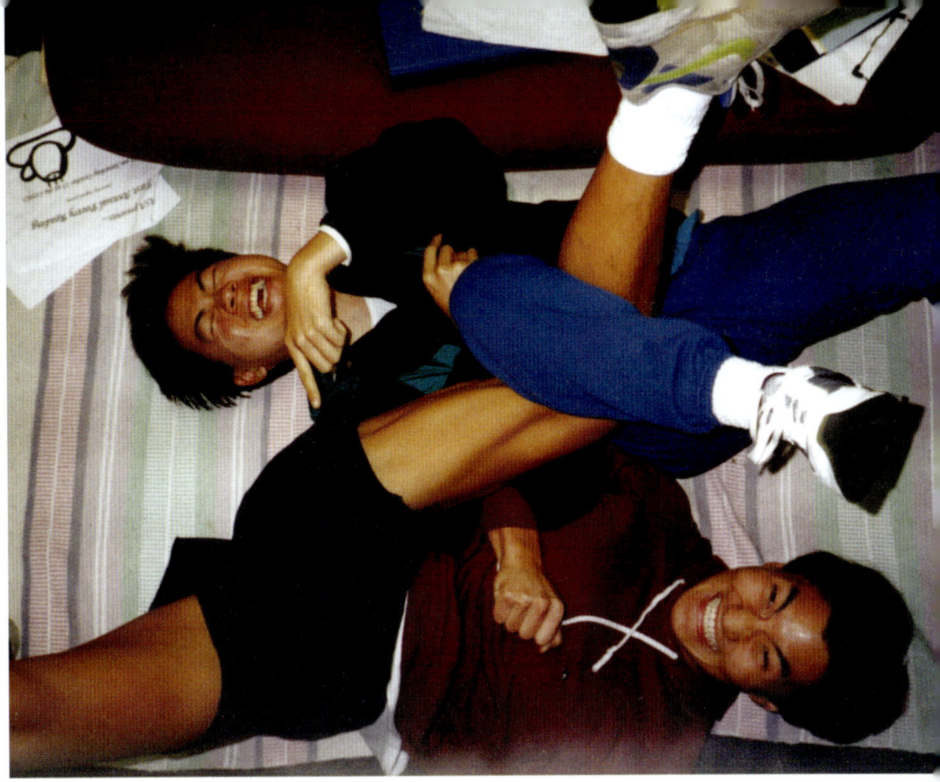

Yul Kwon with his best friend, Evan, whose passing from leukemia inspired his organizing of bone marrow drives. *Courtesy of Yul Kwon*

Yul Kwon as a child.
Courtesy of Yul Kwon

Tyson Apostol (left) facing J.T. Thomas (right) in a brutal challenge during *Survivor: Heroes vs. Villains*. Coach and Jeff Probst look on in the background. *CBS Photo Archive via Getty Images*

Above: John Cochran showing off his *Survivor* passion in his high school yearbook. *Courtesy of John Cochran*
Left: John Cochran in his red vest. *CBS Photo Archive via Getty Images*

Top: Tony Vlachos, perhaps secretly listening in on a conversation. *CBS Photo Archive via Getty Images*

Bottom: Cirie Fields (left) and Zeke Smith (right) connecting during *Survivor: Game Changers*. *CBS Photo Archive via Getty Images*

Zeke Smith performing during his New York improv days. *Courtesy of Zeke Smith*

(Left to right) Kyle Fraser, Shauhin Davari, Joe Hunter, and Kamilla Karthigesu after an unexpected challenge win in *Survivor: 48*. *CBS Photo Archive via Getty Images*

Above: Casting Director Lynne Spillman surrounded by thousands of applications when they were mailed in during the early days of *Survivor* casting. *Courtesy of Lynne Spillman*
Left: Carolyn Wiger with her dog, Kramer.
Courtesy of Carolyn Wiger

Tai Trang

THERE ARE SOME PLAYERS WHO ARE BELOVED FOR HOW strategically they play. Others are favorites because of the big characters they embody. And then there are players who are beloved simply because they are cherishable human beings. That's **Tai Trang**.

A gentle Vietnamese American gardener from San Francisco, Tai arrived on *Survivor: Kaôh Rōng*, the 2016 thirty-second season, with a warmth that cut through the game's usual scheming edge. On that boat marooning stage, he grabbed a chicken for his tribe, a common move in the opening scramble for supplies. His motivations, however, were entirely uncommon. He had no intentions of using the bird as a protein source. "I love all living creatures," he said. He would go on to successfully convince the starving castaways to not eat this chicken and instead, keep him as a pet. He named it Mark and took care of him through the season, ultimately releasing him at an emotional Final Tribal, where Tai was in the running for Sole Survivor. Tai would have a decent resume: finding an idol, winning a challenge, and making it to the finale. But he was a no-vote finalist. Tai's compassion sometimes made him seem naive, but it also made him unforgettable.

At the live reunion, an unexpected voice joined in to celebrate Tai's kindness. In an apparently unplanned moment, pop star Sia—a fan of the show—stood up from the audience and declared her love for Tai. "I could not let Tai go home without saying your authenticity and care for animals really inspired me," she said as a confused Jeff Probst invited her onto the stage and wrapped an arm around her shoulder. She announced a donation of $50,000 for Tai, plus another $50,000 for an animal charity of his choice.

The "Sia Award" would become its own tradition for several seasons—an outside prize awarded to players who Sia chose—typically those who represented some sort of "moral good" in a topical subject. Future recipients were Donathan Hurley, who spoke up about being gay in rural Kentucky and being the caretaker for his grandmother; Aurora McCreary, who told the story of growing up in the foster care system; Janet Carbin, who put strategy aside to support a fellow tribemate during an "unwanted touching" scandal (page 162); and Drea Wheeler, who spoke out about the racial patterns of eliminations.

Suddenly, there was another arbiter of financial success. Not the jury awarding a winner, nor production picking a big character to bring back, but Sia, repeatedly crowning a relevant story year after year. With this award, moral approval became material reward. Being a "good" person in the eyes of Sia, or at least playing one convincingly, now came with financial opportunity. Tai didn't ask for that shift, but he symbolized it: the moment *Survivor*'s social experiment met the logic of celebrity patronage, and telling the right story became currency.

Tai's tenderness, once a liability in the game, became a boon. After two decades of schemers and showmen, the show could now also reward empathy.

Survivor was continuing to be shaped by the world around it—the World Wide Web and pop stars, superfans and performers. And in this new world and media landscape, the reins were slipping, slightly, from production's complete control. As the digital media landscape grew exponentially, for some viewers the act of watching the show transformed from a passive experience to a participatory culture. Fans had the power to influence casting decisions and amplify narratives of their choosing. Players, too, had more agency than ever. They could now interact with audiences directly and build fan communities independent from the show. As their individuality became their strongest asset, they rejected produced archetypes and focused on telling their own stories. For the first time, production was no longer the sole voice in the chorus of *Survivor* and it would have to learn how to become part of the conversation that no longer existed solely on screen.

The Unwritten Rules

Authors of the Story

Zeke Smith

Over the past fifteen years, the world of *Survivor* had learned how to reward performance in all its evolving forms: first strategy, then charm, then spectacle, and finally sincerity. Players had always been the heartbeat of the show, but as *Survivor* looked to regain control of the narrative, it became increasingly invested in *revealing* its players. Confessionals turned into miniature biographies; the great narrators became characters in their own stories. Yet the power to decide which truths to show—how those stories are told— still belonged to the producers. And this shaping of the narrative of someone's life into a tight segment for engaging TV showed just how fragile this line between "character" and "self" could be, how fragile it had always been.

Zeke Smith was a sharp, funny Harvard grad who'd escaped the Great Plains for New York's comedy scene. He had dreamed of being on *Survivor*, playing mock games in Brooklyn. Then, he got cast. At twenty-eight, Zeke was the oldest millennial on the 2016 thirty-third season, *Survivor: Millennials vs. Gen X*. He was there to play a big, bold, fun game—he'd rather go out early swinging big than limp to the end as a goat. He heard the very next season would be a returning player season, and was eager to play a game that would get him a callback from the producers.

That's exactly what he did. On *Millennials vs. Gen X*, Zeke wore a bright, floral Hawaiian shirt—a visual accompaniment to the vibrant game he played. He was a dynamic strategist, a strong narrator. He made fire without flint and won challenges and led blindsides. Smith even led his team into an iconic rock draw—a tiebreaker at Tribal Council where, rather than turn on him, his allies agreed to draw rocks and risk their own elimination. Though he was later voted out, he had played well enough to be asked to return the very next season for *Survivor: Game Changers*.

This superfan had done what he set out to do—he'd earned a spot among the legends he'd once watched from his couch: Sandra Diaz-Twine, Cirie Fields, Tony Vlachos, Ozzy Lusth. He played well again on *Game Changers*, building strong alliances and holding his own among veterans.

Then one moment changed his life forever.

On a sunny afternoon on the sixteenth day on the Mamanuca Islands of Fiji, Zeke's Nuku Tribe lost the Immunity Challenge that ended with a word puzzle: metamorphosis. The loss wasn't fatal to Zeke's game. His alliance held firm, and North Carolina-native Jeff Varner seemed the obvious target.[30] Varner knew he was at risk, telling his tribemates "I'll make my pitch and be at peace." "I would like nothing more than to keep Varner in this game, I like him a hell of a lot as a person," Zeke told his tribe. But he understood this was the practical move they had to make.

Knowing it was likely the last day of Varner's *Survivor* career— "you don't play three times and never make the merge and then get asked back for a fourth season"—Smith paid Varner the respect of letting him know it was likely him on the chopping block tonight. But Varner wasn't "at peace." Instead, he went on a "rampage." In the episode, we see him talk to the other players and tell them Zeke was playing both sides. "He's not being truthful. There's something about Zeke nobody knows," he told them. In his confessional, to producers, he said: "I feel like I know something about Zeke that nobody else has picked up on. It's insignificant to this game, it means

30. Varner had first played in *Australia* and campaigned to get back for *Second Chance*. He had not been a standout player either time, but still, somehow, he got a third chance.

nothing, but this is not the guy you think he is, there's something else here. If I have to go to Tribal tonight and raise mortal hell, I'm going to do it. I'm not going quietly off this island." Presumably producers asked what this big secret he was alluding to was. Whether or not he told them his plans remains a mystery.

At Tribal Council, Varner continued his rampage. "There is deception here," he said, eyes flicking toward Zeke. "Deception on levels these guys don't even understand." Then, almost casually, he turned to Smith: "Why haven't you told anyone you're transgender?"

ZEKE SMITH GREW up in Edmond, Oklahoma, where he was "all kinds of queer" in a place that "wasn't down for that." At Harvard, he expected freedom but found himself still on the margins. "I just already overcame being the weirdo marginalized kid. I came here so I don't have to be that anymore. And now you're saying I don't even fit in with this marginalized population. I'm being segregated to a smaller, marginalized population." It was at college that he learned what being transgender was and "something clearly hit."

Harvard, in the late aughts, was not equipped to help someone who was transitioning and "really struggling mental health-wise." Returning to Oklahoma wasn't an option. Zeke took a year off before his final semester to live in New York City where he found a helpful therapist and underwent top surgery.

It was at this time that Zeke started watching *Survivor* as a bonding activity with his brother who lived in the city and was a fan. "That show's still on?" he initially wondered (like many, he had seen the end of the first season and the beginning of the second, but lost interest). But at this new phase of life, *Survivor* resonated, and quickly, Smith became a fan. "I just remember watching the opening of this pirate ship rocking through the ocean and Probst saying, 'These Americans are about to embark on an adventure that will forever change their lives.'" Zeke, in the midst of a life-changing moment of his own, thought: "I want to become the type of person who could endure *Survivor*, who could be that physically and mentally tough."

As Zeke came to terms with his transition, both physically and emotionally, he worked to become that person. He finished his last semester at Harvard, then moved back to New York and started doing comedy in downtown basements. "I was in a place where I didn't have to tell people I was trans in order to be recognized as who I was," he says. "I was just having such a good time—and was so afraid that if people knew, all this community and joy I'd found would disappear again."

Zeke had long lists of big dreams he'd quietly set aside—running for office, performing on Broadway—anything that would demand disclosure. But he also knew he didn't want to live in fear forever; he wanted to be tough.

"If you were not saddled with the fear," Zeke asked himself, "what would you do?" The answer came to him immediately: he would be on *Survivor*.

Zeke used his "comedy video tricks" to film his audition tape. He built a fire in his Williamsburg backyard, did shirtless push-ups, and spoke directly to the camera about making big, fearless, entertaining moves. Within two hours of submitting the tape, casting called.

He was charming in his interviews. He eventually told producers he was trans—he didn't want it to be a secret—but he made clear he didn't want it to be his *Survivor* story. Zeke didn't want to become "the first trans *Survivor* player"; he just wanted to play the game as himself. Knowing a returning-player season was filming right after, he told producers, "We need to make sure we like each other, 'cause I'm gonna be around all summer."

"I put it into the universe and then manifested it, baby," he says.

As he stepped off the Tribal Council set after his elimination in *Millennials vs. Gen X*, Jeff approached him about playing again—in two weeks. "Can I have a burger, a margarita, and a chance to wipe my ass before I give you an answer?" Zeke joked, but he said yes.

"I was so high on the *Survivor* supply," he says. "So excited, so proud to be there."

In his return on *Game Changers*, Zeke was eager, but the vibes were different this time. He felt the returning players were jaded, sometimes hostile toward production. They were back for business. Some still found his eagerness cute, "like Cirie." (This was the season she'd ultimately be ousted because of all the advantages, page 111). Zeke was playing well again, fully himself, both strategist and storyteller. Then, that moment that changed everything.

When Varner outed Zeke on that sixteenth day, "it was like a bomb dropped in my body," Zeke says. His normally cheery face went blank as the significance of the moment hit him. His tribemates—Ozzy Lusth, Tai Trang, Iowa cop Sarah Lacina, three-time player Andrea Boehlke, and eccentric chemist Debbie Wanner—all sat with him in that moment of shock before coming to his defense, a chorus of voices telling Varner off. Even Jeff Probst looked stunned before reverting to host mode to guide this tricky conversation.

Zeke's first instinct was to run. "But I also had the sense of like, if you go and run, someone is going to come run after you with a camera, and that's not a good look," he says. So he sat in this horrible moment. "Part of the resolve of doing *Survivor* goes back to those origins of wanting to be mentally and emotionally strong. And the thing the mentally and emotionally strong person does is sits and deals with the situation," he says now.

On this heavy night in Fiji, Zeke displayed extraordinary composure. When he was able to find words, he eloquently explained that he had wanted to just play the game as himself—not be minimized to one part of his identity. Then he called back to the puzzle:

If metamorphosis is the word of the episode, I think that I've seen such a metamorphosis of myself over the past—I think today is day fifty-two on Survivor. And I don't know if the scared kid who hit the mat in the marooning in [Season] 33 would be as calm as I am right now, but

I've started two fires with just bamboo, I've won challenges, I've been part of blindsides. I've done all kinds of crazy stuff and I'm a changed, stronger, better man today than I was then. So you know what, Varner, it was really not cool, but you know, I'm fine.

Without the ceremony of a vote, just a verbal agreement from all the players, Varner was eliminated. He hugged Zeke, saying "I'm so sorry." "It's okay man, it's going to be okay," Zeke responded.

With that, and a poignant flair to the tribal music playing in the background, the episode ended.

But the game was still going, the cameras still rolling. "I remember trying to hide in the woods and have a moment to myself but everywhere I went, they were on me," Zeke says. He slept between Sarah and Debbie where he "let out a couple whimpers," but he knew "this is the time to feel whatever feelings you're gonna feel. And then there's no more feeling any feelings."

He stayed in the game for another eleven long days, spiraling, carrying the weight of what had happened. "There was no quiet little off-camera check-in," he says. "No moment of, 'Let's see how your head's doing.'" Strategically, too, his game was effectively over—no one wanted to compete against a story like that in the finale. He was voted out "by the grace of God," on day twenty-nine.

When *Survivor: Game Changers* aired, in spring of 2017, trans rights weren't yet the political flashpoint they would become. Still, this moment rippled far beyond the *Survivor* bubble. Smith understood he might be the first trans person many Americans were knowingly seeing. "I need to handle this in a way that some little trans guy in Oklahoma can watch and be proud," he remembers thinking. But first: "I had this mountain to climb, which was not only preparing for the world to know that I'm trans, but first I had to be okay with being trans myself."

In the months leading up to that episode airing, Zeke felt supported by Jeff Probst and production. They connected him with GLAAD for media training, they covered therapy costs, and Jeff personally read and gave notes on draft-after-draft of Smith's press essays. "There was a feeling among all of us involved just how big this would be," Zeke says. "I had this year of getting ready for *Survivor* and then I had this year of like getting ready for this major thing to happen that was going to change the course of my life."

It did. I ask Zeke about an element I struggle with in telling his story: His *Survivor* game is so much more than the moment of his outing, and he is so much more than this one part of his identity. Zeke didn't want to play *Survivor* and become "the trans *Survivor* player." Yet, how can one tell his *Survivor* story fully, for all of who he is, while acknowledging the significance of this one moment?

"I used to be such a *Survivor* fanboy. I am no longer that person who's super proud of *Survivor*, but I remain super proud of my time on *Survivor* and of my contributions to trans visibility in the world," Zeke says. "So yes, I became 'the trans *Survivor* player.' However, that is the thing I ultimately became more proud of than just, you know, making people go to rocks that one time."

Reflecting on the original impetus for playing—if fear wasn't in the way, what would you do?—Zeke understands now the answer wasn't just *Survivor*. The answer was something he didn't even know was an option at the time: having this experience that would open his life, force him to eliminate that fear. It "made my being trans something I could no longer deny to anyone, anywhere ever again," Smith says.

"It went from me just being a guy who did comedy to . . . I became one of the most visible transgender men in the world," Zeke says. This moment "unlocked the rest of my life." Zeke now serves on GLAAD's board of directors, and, through his work with them, met his husband. "We have a beautiful home and a beautiful puppy."

Through Zeke, *Survivor* was again part of a major cultural moment, and it was garnering a lot of attention from both fans and the media. But that cultural moment also marked a turning point: the moment *Survivor* began mining players' personal lives for cultural relevance in a more explicit way. Smith became a hinge point for *Survivor*—one he is deeply wary of.

The following season, Marine veteran Ben Driebergen (the season's eventual winner) shared his struggles with PTSD. At the reunion, Jeff Probst invoked Zeke by name: "One of the things that I think keeps *Survivor* relevant is that we have new people playing every year, and their stories are 'of the moment' . . . We saw it last year with Zeke and transgender issues, it was a cultural milestone. We had another important story that emerged this season with Ben." Cut to a tight package of the former marine's most vulnerable moments, with stirring music behind it. Like Zeke's, Ben's story was handled with care. But not every player was given the same chance.

A few years later, Zeke got an email from a fellow Harvard alum who was in the *Survivor* casting process. She was asking for advice. His answer was blunt: Don't do it. "You're about to graduate with your second degree . . . an MBA. You already have a job lined up. I didn't have anything else really wonderful going on in my life. You do—and you need to imagine the worst-case scenario."

When the player returned from filming, she called Zeke. "I should have listened to you," she said. "Something bad happened."

THE CALLER WAS Kellee Kim, a business student from California who played on the thirty-ninth season, *Survivor: Island of the Idols*, airing in the fall of 2019.[31]

From day one, Kellee expressed discomfort with multiple instances of unwanted touching from her tribemate, Hollywood executive Dan Spilo. "Dan is a really touchy person," she said in an episode one confessional. "He makes me feel a little bit uncomfortable." All season, the cameras showed him touching the women on his tribe.

31. *Island of the Idols* saw Boston Rob and Sandra Diaz-Twine return as "mentors"—living on a nearby island, complete with giant busts of their heads—advising the players on strategy throughout the season. Jeff Probst has stated that, despite production's offer to build them a shelter, they insisted on reliving the *Survivor* experience in full.

Many of them expressed their discomfort on camera. "It's inappropriate touching. I am not an object," Air Force veteran Missy Byrd said, telling Kellee a story about Dan wiggling her toes while she was in the middle of a conversation with another player.

By the merge, Kellee had had enough. During a confessional to producers, composed but near tears, Kellee explained: "This isn't just one person, it's a [bleep] pattern . . . Yeah, it takes five people to be like the way that I'm feeling about this is actually real, it's not in my head, I'm not overreacting to it. No. He literally has done these things to five different women in this game. That sucks, that totally sucks."

For what appears to be the first time in the show's history, we hear a producer chime in. A male voice off camera: "You know, if there are issues to the point that things need to happen, come to me and I will make sure that stops," he says.

While presumably well-meaning, the producer's interjection failed to acknowledge that significant issues were already happening. Later in the episode, text appeared on screen that said all the players had been spoken to and Dan had been issued a warning. Players have since reported this was a vague meeting about boundaries that didn't speak to the specific issue at hand.

Kellee was one of the season's strongest players and, despite her disgust, tried to separate emotion from strategy. At the merge, she was blindsided, targeted as a big threat with power in the game. She left with two idols in her pocket (and had found three in the game, a record for a female contestant).

The situation with Dan came to a head at the next Tribal Council, where Kellee had to sit silently on the jury, watching as the other contestants debated if these complaints were a "real issue" or just being used for the game. Dan monologued about working in the industry where #MeToo was formed and blossomed and the experience of having a wife and many female employees. If in the "freezing cold rain, or in tight shelters," he did something that made people uncomfortable, he said he apologized.

Fourteen days later, Dan was ejected (not voted off) from the game. An on-screen card explained there had been another incident, off-camera and not involving a player.

Another major cultural moment had crashed onto the shores of *Survivor*, but this time it felt different, gross. Kellee's voice wasn't centered; there was no hopeful-music-backed montage for them to play at the reunion. Kellee watched, silently, from the jury as Dan made himself sympathetic. He would have reached the finale had production not been forced to step in.

At the reunion, Jeff apologized to Kellee, telling her, "Your voice should have been enough." He explained that *Survivor* policies would be changing. In an interview with *The Hollywood Reporter*, Probst sold the season as "one of *Survivor*'s most compelling and socially relevant seasons of all time," adding, "*Survivor* is a microcosm for our real world. Situations just like this one are playing out in offices and bars and colleges across the country and the world." Once again, the players' stories kept this "game of society" culturally relevant—and once again, that relevance came at the expense of the real people who lived them.

"MY STORY AND the way they worked with me is being used to justify them doing this to other people. I can't be a part of that anymore. I can't rubber stamp it, I can't endorse that," Zeke says. He didn't choose to be outed on national television. He made the most out of a situation that never should have happened. Of course, personal stories and clashes have always been core to *Survivor*, from Richard Hatch and Rudy Boesch discussing homosexuality to Sean Rector talking about race with Vecepia Towery. Players naturally bring relevance to the show, and their depiction on screen would always be shaped by their real-life experiences. But what happened to Zeke represented a shift. Cultural relevance would now be put to the forefront on the show itself, players' struggles edited into tight segments and viral-worthy soundbites.

Often on *Survivor* this has been a net positive: Players have used their platforms to highlight a huge range of human experiences—discrimination and domestic violence and addiction and disability. But intentionally bringing these real-world, "of the moment" stories to screens is complicated by who tells their story and how they get told.

"Most people are not naturally oriented toward being activists for whatever their little slice of life is," Zeke says. "Or people come in so excited to tell their story and be advocates for whatever their life experience is, and then they get voted out there and their story never gets told. Or their story doesn't get told in a way that helps them or helps what they're trying to accomplish." Smith's unwarranted outing turned into a "big moment" for *Survivor*—suddenly a show that had not poked through into the cultural zeitgeist in many years, was getting national attention—but it was also a warning flare.

Confronting relevant issues on *Survivor* can become a great platform for sharing a personal story (it can even get you some of Sia's money or an invite back). But the distillate of a single person's story gets shaken with the impacts of the island—with the lens of production, with the chaos of the game—and sometimes that can turn into a dangerous cocktail that no longer tastes like your own truth.

Mike White

SURVIVOR TELLS THE STORY OF SEX AND RACE AND POWER AND money, set against the crashing waves of a tropical island—a brutal struggle of duplicity and schemes, of life and elimination. In *Survivor*, these themes were explored through real people—often for better, sometimes for worse. But soon, parallel—fictional—worlds appeared, worlds in which a master storyteller *can* play with his characters' lives, placing them in dire situations to force out the scandals and stories and themes just below the surface. *Survivor* had spent twenty years creating a saga of its own. Then *Survivor* inspired another Emmy-winning TV show.

Mike White, creator of HBO's *The White Lotus,* appeared on the thirty-seventh season, *Survivor: David vs. Goliath* in 2018, three years before his Emmy-winning drama would captivate audiences.[32]

The season placed players on the David tribe or the Goliath tribe based on the advantages they came to the game with. Mike, who had found Hollywood success writing movies like *School of Rock* and *Nacho Libre,* was a Goliath.

"*Survivor* is a game of social politics that often revolves around the story of the underdog versus the favorite," Jeff Probst said. He

---

32. This wasn't the first time *Survivor* inspired a fictional show. First premiering in Canada before being picked up by Cartoon Network in 2008, *Total Drama Island* was a satirical animated take on *Survivor.* The host, Chris McLean, wears Jeff's signature cargo shirt and necklace combo while many of the "contestants" represented the archetypes made by these legends.

prodded the contestants to share why they might be a David or Goliath. "I grew up in a trailer in the holler," said Nick Wilson, a lawyer from Kentucky. He added, "You know David not only slewed Goliath in the Bible, he ended up becoming a king too. So the story don't stop with David versus Goliath."

Mike played a fantastic game of *Survivor*. He managed his threat level, making savvy social bonds. He orchestrated several blindsides against the season's top players, he won challenges, and even won the Final Four Fire-Making to secure his spot at the finale. It was there, however, that Nick's prescient comments came true. That David "slewed" Goliath Mike, who came in second place in a 7-3-0 vote.

Mike has said he regrets not pushing harder at the Final Tribal Council. "The David–Goliath theme made me feel like everyone wanted a David to win, and this whole season would be a giant letdown—for production, for CBS, for America—if the Hollywood Goliath secures the bag," he told *Entertainment Weekly*. "Although everyone knows in real life, the Goliath always wins—and by letting a David win, we're just perpetuating the hollow American myth that the 'little guy', through wile and determination, can overcome all the obstacles of a rigged system. Look around, people—the rich get richer! So let's not peddle fantasies that keep us from dismantling structures of economic oppression."

This sentiment would carry over from one Pacific island to another. The first season of *The White Lotus*, set in Hawaii, saw the dynamics between the David hotel employees and Goliath guests. In *The White Lotus*, unlike *Survivor*, the Goliaths won—like they usually do. The rich and powerful stayed rich and powerful.

Beyond the thematic reckoning, Mike, as a fan and then player, was inspired by his fellow castaways, the human beings pushed to their limits. "The first season of *Survivor*, these people were, like, straight out of life. So funny and complex. And also very base and human," he told *Vulture*. "You see how people bungle having power, how the oppressed becomes the oppressor, the bully becomes the bullied." To *The New Yorker* he added: "I aspire to do what reality television already does. To create characters that are surprising and dimensional and do weird shit and capture your attention."

For Mike, playing *Survivor* wasn't just about competing on a show he loved: It became a research trip for the vivid and unique characters he would come to create on *The White Lotus*.[33] Season 50 is another research trip for Mike, a second chance to make his case—and perhaps we'll see Cirie Fields as a guest at the White Lotus hotels soon.

While this Goliath didn't win his season, the 20s and 30s of *Survivor* still saw players who became behemoths during their appearances—and still took home the win.

33. As of the third season of *The White Lotus*, six players from Mike's season—two Davids and four Goliaths—have made cameos on the award-winning drama. Look for them lounging by the pool and ordering drinks at beachside bars.

Kim Spradlin, Natalie Anderson & Jeremy Collins

FIFTEEN YEARS INTO *SURVIVOR*, MOST OF THE GAME'S GREAT experiments had already been run. Idols and blindsides were routine, alliances shifted hourly, and returning players had redrawn the map and built their legacies. It was easy to believe the age of a single, dominant player was over—that the game had become too self-aware, too fractured, for one person to steer the ship completely.

And yet, a few winners reminded us that the concept of dominance hadn't vanished; it had simply evolved. Kim Spradlin, Natalie Anderson, and Jeremy Collins each found ways to control the game without breaking its social fabric—to be trusted, even when they were in charge. Their wins revealed what the modern jury had come to value: composure, timing, empathy, and a kind of visible decency that made ambition feel moral.

On *Survivor*'s twenty-fourth season, airing in 2012, **Kim Spradlin** played what many consider one of the most flawless winning games on the show. It wasn't a "perfect" game, number-wise, like that of J.T. Thomas and John Cochran, but it was dominant socially, strategically, and physically.

A bridal shop owner from Texas, Spradlin has high cheekbones, striking blue eyes, and a nose that the eccentric plastic surgeon on her season, Tarzan Smith, deemed "perfect." She carried herself with an easy calm and an understated confidence, a poise that made her seem both approachable and untouchable.

From the start, Kim built alliances that ran in multiple directions, making herself essential to everyone. "This has been my thing all along. I'm trying to keep my options open," she said. She had a universal belovedness that hadn't been seen since J.T. (and also like J.T., she was voted the player others would trust with their life in the Touchy Subjects challenge). Like Cirie Fields, she found herself as the social core of the tribe, with information coming to her from all sides. Like Ethan Zohn, opponents would try to emphasize her likability and threat level, but her allies wouldn't turn against her. Like Parvati Shallow, she was a force in winning challenges. In fact, Kim holds the tied record for most immunity wins by a female contestant, at four (tied with Kelly Wiglesworth from Season 1, Rachel Lamont, who won Season 47, and others).

Kim came to *Survivor* on the heels of a divorce. Her season's starting tribes were split by gender. While she wooed plenty of the men into thinking they were allies, the alliance she ultimately went to the end with was all women. By Final Tribal, she was one of the most obvious winners in *Survivor* history, claiming the title in a 7–2–0 vote. Kim showed that even in a modern era filled with twists and paranoia, it was still possible to run a season with calm, controlled mastery.

NATALIE ANDERSON ARRIVED on the beaches of *Survivor: San Juan del Sur* with determination and a competitive spirit. She was loud, strong, and fearless. In a show often hellbent on putting its players into neat, identity-defined boxes, she played the game in a way no woman (and particularly no woman of color) had—or, rather, had been allowed to. With a ferocity and physicality, profanity and aggression, she played a game that defied the expectations of her gender, unapologetically.

Natalie Anderson entered the show's twenty-ninth season in 2014 alongside her twin Nadiya on this *Blood vs. Water* themed season. The Sri Lankan American sisters—shockingly, the first South Asians ever cast, twenty-nine seasons into the show's run—had already competed together on *The Amazing Race*. Their bond was obvious; outside of the game, they lived together and had never been apart. But when Nadiya was the first player voted out, Natalie was left to play on her own. She cried when she got the news (reportedly her first cry in a decade), but rallied, explaining that—"now it's just really good motivation to keep my head in the game." She did.

Natalie responded to her twin's elimination not by shrinking into the background, but by playing louder, sharper, and more ferociously than anyone else. She was fiery and unafraid to show emotion, calling out allies publicly when they seemed to be wavering. In an iconic moment, she famously yelled across Tribal Council, "Did you vote for who I told you to vote for?" to her ally, Jaclyn, before promptly playing an idol to save her. It has become one of the most famous shouts in the show's history.

Beneath the volume was calculation. She orchestrated smart moves and balanced being both passionate and trustworthy, calling out bullshit while remaining reliable. Ultimately, what made Natalie's game so dangerous was her timing. She let others flame out early, then surged in the late game, targeting those tied to both her sister's ousting and the blindside of her closest ally, Jeremy, carving a path of vengeance that also doubled as strategy. Winning 5-2-1 (and basically only not receiving the votes of the family members of her opponents) Anderson showed that a winner could be brash and openly confrontational—and still be dominant. Hers wasn't a quiet, subtle mastery, but a storm: loud, forceful, and unstoppable once it picked up speed.

In winning, Natalie became the first Asian woman to win, and only the third woman of color after Vecepia Towery and Sandra Diaz-Twine. Hers wasn't a win that played into expectations of her gender, but one that blatantly defied them, dominating the competition while still remaining celebrated.

JEREMY COLLINS, NATALIE'S closest ally who was blindsided in *San Juan del Sur,* returned for his second chance in *Survivor's* thirty-first season, *Cambodia: Second Chance*, an obvious pick in the fan vote. Like his fellow players, **Jeremy Collins** returned to the game with unfinished business and a sharpened approach. Even among this star-studded cast of players out for vengeance, the Massachusetts firefighter stood out. Collins also carried a secret motivation—his wife Val was pregnant during filming—and he rooted his game in that drive.

What set Jeremy apart was his ability to combine strength with warmth. He was the guy everyone trusted, the ally you wanted in your corner, even as he was quietly shaping the season around him—not through flashy gameplay or manipulation, but through real connections.

Strategically, Jeremy named, perfected, and solidified as lore one of *Survivor*'s most important modern tactics: the "meat shield" strategy. Knowing his physical presence made him a threat, he surrounded himself with other big targets like Joe Anglim, a challenge threat considered to be the second coming of Ozzy Lusth, and Andrew Savage, the striking, likable lawyer who had been Pagong'ed out in Sandra's first season, *Pearl Islands*. By aligning with and hiding behind these more obviously threatening "alpha men," Jeremy managed his own threat level. He also found and correctly played two hidden idols, not just to save himself but to protect his allies (in this case, J.T. Thomas's BFF and Rob Cesternino's fellow Know-it-All, Stephen Fishbach). He was calm at camp and loyal in his bonds, rarely letting paranoia creep into his relationships.

Jeremy had dominance without flash. He built a gradual accrual of goodwill through smart strategy, loyalty, and likability. He played the game with as much honor as possible. And in his final speech to the jury, Collins explained his game with clarity, and revealed the secret motivator of his whole game: his soon-to-come third child. It was a son, his wife had revealed to him during the family visit. That was enough to see Jeremy win in a unanimous vote, with an argument to be made for that numerically "perfect" game, given the only votes ever cast against him were negated by his idol play.

Kim, Natalie, and Jeremy each returned for the fortieth season, *Winners at War.* Each maintained the strengths that had once defined them. Kim still radiated calm, Natalie, fight, and Jeremy, trust. All three played well, but none could bend the game entirely to their will—because one player proved undeniably dominant.

Tony Vlachos

EVERY SEASON, THE JURY OF *SURVIVOR* PICKS THE WINNER that represents their game. In choosing who they see as the most deserving of the win, this jury of "ordinary people" gives insight into what they value, reflecting some combination of contemporary societal values and the expectations of reality TV. Fatefully, Sue Hawk picked the snake (Richard Hatch) over the rat (Kelly Wiglesworth). The *Cook Islands* jury picked Yul Kwon's considered strategy over Ozzy Lusth's physical dominance. The women of *Micronesia* chose to celebrate Parvati Shallow's relentlessness. And time and time again, juries told Russell Hantz he had gone too far.

In winning not once, but twice, **Tony Vlachos** became one of the great barometers of these evolving norms of the jury and solidified his standing as one of the greatest players of the game.

TONY GREW UP in Jersey City, New Jersey. "While we weren't fortunate enough to live in the life of luxuries, we had what fortune couldn't buy: love, values, and good morals," he says. That structure guided him into a career as a police officer—one where, he says, his mission was less about "catching the bad guy" than about helping people who needed it most.

But long before donning the badge, Vlachos had already learned how to think strategically, how to outwit. He remembers buying chips as a kid and, after sharing them with friends, realizing he'd been left with "only two or three chips" for himself. "So in no time at all, I figured out the chips my buddies did not like, and strategically bought those chips where I got to eat the whole bag." He assembled a bicycle from junk parts, but hacked it so his friends wouldn't want to borrow it. "The handlebar had to be turned far left [for the bike] to go straight. None of my buddies wanted to put the effort into figuring out how to ride the bike with this 'improvement,' so they never asked to borrow it, and I would ride my crooked handlebar bike all day without having to give it up to anyone."

Tony has always been someone who anticipates. "My mind would always try to think a few steps ahead of what the next person might be thinking." This instinct to create edges others didn't see became his trademark on the show.

Tony hadn't been interested in watching *Survivor*. He figured it was "just a survivalist show." It wasn't until a friend made him watch an episode (he doesn't remember which, but it was "an episode with Russell Hantz") that he learned "it's not about survivalists, it's a ruthless backstabbing game!" He went back through the catalog and binged every season.

Vlachos cites inspiration from watching characters like Richard, Sandra, Russell, Coach, Tyson, and more. "I would laugh in tears one second, and the other, I would be at the edge of my seat asking myself, 'How are they pulling this off?'"

Tony was eager to apply and knew the gameplay would come naturally to him. "I was dealing with this same game out on the streets for $100k a year," he says, "so I figured, let me try winning ten years of my salary in just thirty-nine days for doing the same things."

When Tony first got the call from *Survivor*'s producers, he thought it was a friend playing a prank. "I was pretty cold and standoff-ish." Then he realized it was real. "I completely changed my tune and was screaming with joy," he says.

"That's why we love you," the casting producer told him. "You are a multi-dimensional person who just went from supercold to superhot within a millisecond."

Despite the casting success, Tony's *Survivor* dreams had to wait.

He was enlisted for Season 25, but the filming overlapped with his wedding, so he pulled himself from the process. "You're welcome, Denise!" he jokes to that season's winner, Denise Stapley. Eventually, he was called back for *Survivor: Cagayan,* the twenty-eighth season premiering in 2014.

Tony hit the beaches of Cagayan like a storm and became one of the most fun players to watch. He built a "Spy Shack" to eavesdrop on his teammates, gracing screens with stunning shots of him peeking out through palm fronds. He scrambled for idols (and found them) and kept his game moving at a frenetic pace.

Vlachos entered *Cagayan* telling everyone he worked in construction, not that he was a cop. But five minutes into the show, fellow police officer, Sarah Lacina, claimed he set off her "cop-dar." He doubled down at first, but soon confessed, forming a Cops-R-Us Alliance with her—swearing his allegiance on his badge. Unfortunately for Sarah, in the game of *Survivor,* Tony didn't care about his badge. "She had me swear on my badge. That doesn't mean anything to me, swearing on my badge. Because I'm here to lie, cheat and steal. I'm here to drag people's dreams through the mud so I can pursue mine. That's what I'm here for. It's as simple as that," he explained in a confessional.

Tony relished his lies. Having watched players like Richard and Sandra, he understood them as an essential element of the game. "I watched many seasons of *Survivor* before going out to play, and the one thing the greatest players on the show had in common was lies. Lies, lies and more lies," he says. "It's very difficult for a genuinely good person to look someone in the eyes and promise them something they know isn't true. Especially when . . . you are sleep deprived, food deprived, dehydrated and you just need someone to open up to and trust. So to be able to shut all that down and go against your natural being, is usually the difference between losing and winning this game."

Tony sees lying not as a morally questionable means to an end, but as a hard-to-master but essential tool, necessary to playing a winning game.

What separated Tony's lies and chaos from someone like Russell Hantz before him is that his duplicity was elastic and intentional, not spiteful—aimed at the vote, not the person. Tony's game never felt cruel. He was sincerely friendly to his tribemates and helpful around camp. He would stay up all night to keep the fire burning (while also using the time to work through every possible strategic scenario in his head). He would never throw socks into it.

"Just because I wanted to beat my opponents didn't mean I wanted them to have a miserable time out there in those brutal conditions," Vlachos says. This understanding meant he could befriend his fellow players, keep them laughing in camp, and then lie straight to their face and vote them out that night. Amidst the betrayals, he was goofy, high-energy, and relentlessly entertaining—a player who seemed to love the absurdity of *Survivor* even as he broke hearts within it.

In Cagayan, Tony tore through any relationship he had. His efforts took him to the final three and, in another season with just a two-person Final Tribal, martial arts instructor Woo Hwang chose to take Tony to the end with him over the jury-reviled Kass McQuillen.[34] It was a noble move, *a la* Colby Donaldson, with Woo explaining: "If I take someone like Kass and break my loyalty to Tony, it completely contradicts who I am, and I become the biggest hypocrite." In the jury's hands was a battle between Woo's loyalty and Tony's dominance through almost-constant disloyalty.

At Final Tribal, it was clear the jury members had been waiting for their moment to tear through Tony. One after the other, eliminated players used their airtime to question his integrity, to see if he fessed up to the lies. "I want you to own your game and admit that you were the villain," former Miss Kentucky Teen USA Jefra Bland

---

34. A memorable character in her own right, she gave herself the nickname "Chaos Kass" while on the show. She fully embraced her unpredictable style of gameplay—flipping on alliances, blindsiding allies, and generally sowing chaos. She returned one year later in *Survivor: Cambodia*, but was eliminated after the merge.

pressed. "I am owning it, Jefra," Tony responded, adding that he was "half villain, half good player . . . I was just doing strategic moves to save myself."

Tribal culminated with his once-closest ally Trish Hegarty, a Massachusetts Pilates trainer, taking a cue from the Sue Hawk school of blistering, epic Final Tribal speeches. She recounted, in front of her fellow jury members, how Tony had sworn on his father's grave that he wouldn't turn on her.

"I have a one-million-dollar question for you that I want you to answer," Hegarty asked, torchlight flickering in the background. "Was it worth it to you, for a million dollars, to sacrifice your own father to get you here?" Tony began trying to explain himself, but Trish butted in. She didn't want excuses: "Yes or no. It's a million-dollar question."

"Yes," Tony answered.

The jury voted and Tony won, getting eight of the nine possible votes. The values were clear.

Tony mostly received love after this win. "True fans got it," he says. Twenty-eight seasons in, this kind of fun and ruthless gameplay was celebrated, especially coming from someone who looked and played like Tony.

NOT MUCH CHANGED in his life after the win, except that "comparing milk and egg prices at the supermarket was a thing of the past."

Tony was called back a few years later to play on *Game Changers*. He sprinted into the jungle searching for an idol on day one, and was gone by day six. The takeaway: "Maybe if there is a next time, I have to lean away from the *Cagayan* Tony and not lean into it."

That next chance came with *Winners at War*. The show's fortieth season and twentieth anniversary featured an all-winners cast—a roster that read like *Survivor*'s Avengers: Boston Rob, Sandra Diaz-Twine, Parvati Shallow, Yul Kwon, Tyson Apostol, Kim Spradlin alongside Tony.[35] With the first confessional of the season, Vlachos explained: "Fans of football wait all year to see the Super Bowl. Fans of *Survivor* have waited twenty years to see *Winners at War*."

This time, he came in anew. "It was more important for me to start the game as me. As a person, not as a player," he says. He created bonds over parenthood and formed connections in the quiet "real-life" talks with other players, remembering to keep his threat level low.

Still, he delivered the same energetic, entertaining TV. This time, instead of a "Spy Shack," there was a "Spy Nest" where he hid up in the trees to listen in on other players' conversations. He did his fair share of lying and scheming, scrambling for idols and orchestrating game-changing blindsides. He brought back the Cops-R-Us Alliance with Sarah Lacina (who had won *Game Changers*), but this time he stayed loyal all the way until the Final Four Fire-Making, where he dramatically beat her, ending in an emotional embrace with Sarah comforting a teary-eyed Tony. He played *Survivor* hard, but played with heart. He also won four challenges in the process.

At a rainy Final Tribal Council, the final three players made their cases to the jury. Michelle Fitzgerald, the winner of Season 32, *Kaoh Rong*, explained she was always on the outs and had to fight to stay in the game. Natalie Anderson (page 170), the powerhouse from *San Juan Del Sur*, had been the first player eliminated and used her physical strength to win her way back from the "Edge of Extinction."

Tony explained his game—how he knew when to hold back and when to throw punches. He had the jury laughing out loud as he described the Spy Nest, and impressed the greats with his

---

35. Notably, Tina Wesson and Vecepia Towery were missing. The OG winner, Richard Hatch, was meant to be there, but after production fumbled the ball with Kellee's experience the season prior, they didn't want to remind viewers of the history between Richard and Sue Hawk.

performance. Parvati and Boston Rob asked how he managed to blindside so many people without leaving them feeling burned and resentful. "The bonds were real," he told them. He said the connections they made as human beings were not just about strategy—they were meaningful to him. But the lies, he felt, were how you win. He had to be both a human being and a game player. "I know it's a big, huge Super Bowl season of *Survivor* and I tried my best to be a great player for the season, and I hope you guys can appreciate the hard work I put into it to get to where I am tonight," he said.

Over a Zoom reunion, amidst the COVID uncertainty of May 2020, Jeff Probst read out the votes. Tony won 12-4-0, over Natalie and Michelle, respectively. He won the $2 million prize and became the second two-time winner in *Survivor* history.

His was the game this jury awarded. And it wasn't just a jury of strangers, but a jury of winners: a group of legends who understand what it takes to win this game.

THE QUESTION OF how to play *Survivor* has always been a central tension of the show. The lack of explicit rules is a large part of what makes the game so compelling, and a winning strategy in one season may be a complete disaster in the next. How do you build meaningful bonds while backstabbing your allies? How much manipulation and scheming and lying is worth it for the ultimate prize? And how do you portray yourself on screen while trying to entertain audiences and manipulate the game in your favor? It is the core question Kelly Wiglesworth asked in the very first season: "How do you stay true to yourself and maintain integrity and still play this game?" In *Winners at War*, a jury of legends provided an answer by rewarding the unique combination of strategy and sincerity that underscored not just Tony's wits, but his performance—his game and his character.

That winning character was something Tony seemed able to maintain narrative control over. Some players like Tina Wesson, J.T. Thomas, and John Cochran actively leaned into their assigned roles for a chance at success. Others, like Parvati Shallow and Cirie Fields, played their roles but defied the expectations of them. Still others like Sean Rector, Yul Kwon, and Zeke Smith navigated the stereotypes and narratives that might shape the expectations of their character. Tony, meanwhile, played the game as himself. His gender, race, and charismatic personality let him command both his "character" and his "self," free from others' preconceived ideas about how he should play or who he should be. "That fun, goofy energetic character, that's exactly who I am in life," he says.

Vlachos could be completely himself when building real-world connections. "Talking about family formed genuine bonds, where you temporarily get lost into a much-needed safe and euphoric space," he says. "The genuine talks we have out there in the jungle are sincere . . . [the relationships] last much longer than the lies and blindsides," Tony says.

"But as we know, all good things do come to an end," Tony says. He knew when to turn off the caring "self," and when to turn on the masterful player.

Like many who have won the game, Tony understands that ruthlessness is a necessary part of it, as established by Richard Hatch and proven by players like Parvati or Boston Rob. "On a soccer field you kick the ball. On a basketball court you shoot the ball. On a baseball field, you hit the ball with a bat. On *Survivor* you lie, backstab, and blindside your opponents. That is the game," Tony says. It echoes the sentiment Hatch voiced—"A football player doesn't tap his opponent on his shoulder and say, 'Hey, I'm about to tackle you.' He fucking plows him."

This mentality made Hatch a villain, but twenty years into *Survivor*—twenty years into so many fantastic, ruthless, cunning players shaping the show and the genre with it, shaping the norms of what is acceptable in this game of society—it could be celebrated.

Tony played the ultimate season of *Survivor*. Because of who he is and how he presented himself, audiences and fellow players alike honored his win. And with this, his jury of peers etched into stone those unwritten rules of how to acceptably play this game.

CHAPTER 6

Come On In

A Welcome to a New Era

Ricard Foyé

IT WAS FALL OF 2021, AND RICARD FOYÉ WAS GETTING READY
for the premiere of his season of *Survivor*—the forty-first. It had been
a long time coming. For the first time in its more than twenty-year
history, *Survivor* took a year and a half off from production during
the COVID-19 pandemic. The previous season, *Winners at War,* was
a culmination of the old ways. Now *Survivor* was beginning a "New
Era"—a game restructured, with fewer days (twenty-six instead of
thirty-nine), new twists, and updated rules.[36]

Ricard Foyé had gone through the extensive casting process, then
through an extended quarantine in both California and Fiji. He had
gone out and played *Survivor* and waited. Now premiere day was
here, he was ready: "I'm so excited. People are about to see me live
my dream."

He was hosting a watch party at a bar in Seattle. Ricard's friends
and family were there (including friend and fellow Washingtonian,
Kelley Wentworth), all excited to watch the first episode. As they
were setting up the TV, Ricard got a call from an unknown number.

"I'm a weirdo," he says. "I actually answer my phone to phone
numbers that I don't recognize." When Foyé picked up his phone,
the caller said: "Fuck you, you should die," then promptly hung up.

36. Longtime casting director Lynne Spillman was also out. "It was the best
thing that could have happened," she says. After decades of devoting her life to
finding the incredible figures who shaped the game, she needed to devote time
to her family, her friends, and travel.

Confused, Ricard opened Twitter to see countless posts calling him all sorts of offensive names.

The first episode hadn't even started airing in Seattle, but it had already concluded on the East Coast, and clearly he had done something to deeply anger some fans. But he had no idea what it was. "So now I had to spend two hours freaking out, 'cause I did not know why I was the most hated person on the cast," he tells me. "It was one of the worst nights I could have imagined." Ricard watched and waited, anxious to see what could have warranted the instantaneous online backlash.

The episode started as they often do: shots of the new castaways looking out at the horizon as they rode on speed boats toward a large ship for their marooning. Interspersed were early confessionals—the players introducing themselves and sharing their excitement, the importance of *Survivor* in their life, the way they planned on approaching the game. Nothing from Ricard yet.

When they reached the ship, Jeff Probst began his usual chatter with the contestants. Then he opened the door to those moments of cultural relevance, now especially pertinent amidst the churning waters of social change in 2021 America: "As we all know we are in the midst of one of the most powerful, still-evolving periods of time that we will probably ever go through in our lives," Jeff said to the castaways. "While you're out there backstabbing, blindsiding, swearing on kids that you may or may not really have, if something comes up that you want to talk about, talk about it. Who knows, we might learn something."

Then Probst led by example: "I'll start, because I need your guidance on something. For twenty years I have used one phrase to call people in for challenges." He pointed to the castaways, who yelled in unison, "Come on in, guys!"—validating the significance of this line in *Survivor* lore.

"Love saying it, it's part of the show," Jeff said. "But I, too, want to be of the moment. So my question to you to decide for us . . . is a word like 'guys' okay, or is it time to retire that word?"

Another contestant, Evvie Jagoda, raised her hand. She said that as a queer woman, she had no qualms. Jeff asked if anyone disagreed, but the other players stayed silent. Probst looked straight into the camera: "Okay, mark it down. Discussed and decided." Case closed.

For Ricard, these early minutes of the game were chaotic. After years of waiting and weeks of quarantining, alone and silent, they had taken off their masks and suddenly the cameras were rolling, the show was starting. "And I just remember thinking, why is he asking us this? Why is this the very beginning of the game? This group of eighteen people, we should not be the voice of how the game should be played."

Ricard was quiet during the initial marooning, still processing his surroundings and wrapping his head around being on the show. But as the hours passed, he reflected more on the question Jeff asked. Ricard didn't personally have a problem with "guys" used to address a group, regardless of gender. But he felt the responsibility that was being placed in the hands of the players with this decision. Ricard is gay. He knew his husband at the time, who is a trans man, did have an opinion on gendered language. He thought about the queer youth camp he volunteers at in the summers—a place that was integral to shaping his acceptance of himself—and the inclusive values he tries to instill there.

"I'm there teaching them constantly to think about how they speak to other people. And here I am on national television, not saying a word about it," Foyé says. If the decision came down to the players, why not choose the most inclusive option?

At the first challenge, Probst welcomed the players in with the now-approved "Come on in, guys." Ricard decided to speak up. He said there was so much going on during the marooning, and "I didn't have the capacity to do what I'm really supposed to do, which I regret."

Ricard told Jeff that he didn't agree with using "guys" to address everyone. "I fully agree we should change it . . . the reality is *Survivor* has changed over the last twenty-one years, and those changes have allowed all of us, all of these brown people, Black people, Asian people, so many queer people to be here simultaneously."

Jeff responded with his usual cheeriness: "I'm with you, I want to change it," adding, "I love that. We just made a change; from now on it is 'Come on in.'"

In that instant, *Survivor* made both a change and a sound bite: real reform, captured in real time.

This was the moment that caused Ricard to get the threatening phone call and the onslaught of hate posts online. It's the moment that led to the regular death threats he still receives, to the people coming up to him on the street and telling him he ruined the show, to the absurd hand-delivered package he received at his front door containing shredded photos of him and a Christmas card scrawled with terrible insults. In the years since his appearance on the show, Ricard has started taking anxiety medication; he still struggles going into public.

Twenty years earlier, Richard Hatch had faced death threats for introducing duplicity and effectively birthing the game. Now, Ricard faced a similar backlash—not for affecting the gameplay in any major way, but for a singular moment, suggesting the reconsideration of a single word. In 2021, the United States was a far more polarized country—due, in large part, to that same connected internet that also gave fans a voice. Ricard became the face of a game changed— and a scapegoat for those who saw that progress as a threat.

RICARD REMEMBERS WATCHING the first season of *Survivor* with his mom. "I lived in a household where, if there was a show or a movie with a gay character, my family would just turn it off. That's just what it was," he says.

But while watching *Survivor*, his mom (probably in the minority for the time) loved Richard Hatch; she was rooting for him. "I had never seen her rooting for a gay person, a gay character, anything. But she loved this guy. She loved how real he was. It didn't matter that he was gay." Ricard, ten years old at the time, didn't yet have the language to come out, but it was in this seed of *Survivor*'s representation and Richard Hatch's brave openness, that a hope of acceptance blossomed in a young Ricard: "My mom could potentially root for me as a gay person."

Ricard had long wanted to apply for the show, but the timing was never quite right. As a young adult, he began touring as a dancer. Then he became a flight attendant, and early in his career, didn't have much freedom to take off time from work. He later got married and had a child.

It was Valentine's Day in 2020 and Ricard, now a senior flight attendant, had forgotten to ask for the holiday off. He was in a hotel room, watching *Survivor* on his laptop and wishing he could be home celebrating with his husband. "I am not a drinker. It is so rare that I drink," he says. But it was Valentine's Day, so why not have a bottle of wine? Soon, he was quite drunk.

"I took my phone and in one take I made a three-minute-long video being like, 'Jeff, I'm gonna be on *Survivor*. I'm your brown guy. I am gay. I have a trans husband. That's crazy,'" Ricard says, with an impressive impression of a drunken slur. He went on to describe how he would play the game by lowering his threat level, making close allies, and proving helpful in challenges. "I was just rambling on. But they called me."

Behind the scenes, something else was happening. *Winners at War* had tied the bow on a previous era of the show. COVID had halted production (there was an original cast for Season 41, set to depart in March of 2020). Former players were using this pause, and the momentum of national movements like Black Lives Matter, to advocate for changes to *Survivor*. Sean Rector, Zeke Smith, Kellee Kim, and countless other alumni were in conversations with CBS, pushing for a more just production of a show they both appreciated and criticized. A former player from *Cagayan*, J'Tia Hart, and an organization of Black *Survivor* alumni—The Soul Survivors—led a petition for at least 30 percent of the cast to be people of color, as well as increased representation on the production side, and better access to mental health resources for players.

CBS responded and, in some ways, over-delivered. The network announced an initiative to have their reality TV casts be made up of at least 50 percent people of color. Less specifically, *Survivor* production said it would seek to have better diversity behind the camera, and improve LGBTQ representation.

When Ricard was cast, he didn't know he was part of this New Era diversity push. Players weren't told about new rules—even the shortened game—until just before the season began filming. But, in many ways, Ricard became an unexpected face of the change. He is gay and brown, of Puerto Rican descent. He was a father married to a trans husband. While filming, he had another child on the way. He is hard of hearing, deaf in his right ear, and was proud to represent the hard of hearing community on the show. He represented groups not always represented on the show.

Ricard played a great game. He was on a pre-merge disaster tribe but became one of only two players to survive it. He built strong relationships, shaped strategy, and won an impressive three Immunity Challenges. Eventually he was eliminated at the final five, right before fire-making, since he was seen as the biggest threat to win.

Ricard's edit on *Survivor* was nuanced. His identity didn't define his game but certainly influenced it. Late in the game, on the ninth episode, a short sequence featured muffled audio to mimic his perspective. It wasn't sonically accurate to how he hears, but Ricard appreciated the moment. He spoke in a confessional about his hearing loss—how he was originally anxious about it but has found it advantageous to read lips and sense body language. Ricard got to tell this piece of his story. But his existence also helped *Survivor* tell a story they wanted to showcase.

Ricard noticed questions during confessional interviews that opened "opportunity for me to discuss being the brown guy, being the gay guy, the trans family. It came up more often than I ever would've brought it up myself," he says.

An early preview clip for the season showed Ricard saying, "I want to be the first brown, gay, hard of hearing winner. That would be really special to me." Ricard did say this, but it wasn't truly his focus. "That was not a priority to me at all going out there." He says, "It had nothing to do with being gay or brown. I did wanna be a hard of hearing winner. That was really cool to me, to overcome a very real thing that could be difficult in the show. Being gay isn't difficult in the show, in my opinion. Being brown isn't that difficult in the show."

In this cultural moment of 2021, *Survivor* wanted to prove it had listened and evolved, and it leaned on Ricard's mere existence on the show as its proof.

The "come on in, guys" moment was the cherry on top for the show to preform its evolution. It played as the perfect gesture: quick, symbolic, easy to interpret. Ricard didn't think the moment would even make the episode; he thought it was a production note. But of course it aired. It made *Survivor* look aware without the production taking responsibility for the change themselves. That burden fell on Ricard, who became the symbol—and, later, the target—of the New Era's "progressive" shift.

Ricard hadn't come on *Survivor* to be an activist. He knew what he represented, but didn't want that to define him. When he arrived and saw the diversity around him, he felt relief: "Oh, there's a lot of queens here. That's cool. I can actually be more myself because I'm not the only one." That's the promise of the New Era: increased diversity meant that once-stereotyped players could just be themselves. And for Ricard, his edit in full reflected that with a complex and multi-dimensional story. The game was changing, and often beautifully so.

But still, that one scene—just a single word—became the emblem of all those changes. And for those who decry a "woke" *Survivor*, Ricard was the easy scapegoat.

Maryanne Oketch
& Jesse Lopez

THROUGH ITS EARLIEST SEASONS, THE CENTRAL FRAMING OF *Survivor* was heroes versus villains. It was storytelling at its simplest: good versus evil. This was once presented like a clear line in the sand—cue the scheming Richard Hatch versus the noble Colby Donaldson. But individuals are, of course, far more complex than that. As players increasingly understood their role as performers and recaptured control over their branding, there were waves of new stories crashing up on that line between good and evil, blurring and redefining it.

In the New Era, this line blurred even further. The post-Tony Vlachos world solidified the essential nature of duplicity. Now everyone was showing up on the island ready to get scheming—in fact, you'd be criticized if you didn't. The edits of players' stories now often invoked a fuller person, beyond simple archetypes, making it harder to villainize individual castaways. Plus, the growing specter of social media backlash meant players were more aware than ever of how their every move was being judged by millions of viewers each week. Kindness could be strategy, and betrayal could make compelling television. The simple story of good versus evil was nowhere to be found.

MARYANNE OKETCH LEAPED into Season 42 as a ball of sunlight—laughing at her own jokes, talking too fast, and exuding the kind of open, guileless joy *Survivor* had trained viewers to underestimate.

Her exuberance was a lot to take in. Tribemates rolled their eyes. She knew it and leaned into it. But beneath the bubbliness and long-winded stories was calculation. **Maryanne Oketch** found two idols and a secret advantage. While many overlooked her as comic relief, she was quietly orchestrating her endgame. She even organized the blindside of her closest ally and biggest threat, Omar Zaheer, using her extra vote to knock him out with a brilliantly brutal 3-2-2 plurality. When, at Final Tribal, she revealed a secret hidden idol she never had to use—after playing a game no one thought she was capable of—her jury was stunned. They rewarded her, in a 7-1-0 vote, not just for surviving, but for subverting their expectations. She became the second Black woman, after Vecepia Towery, to win the game.

Maryanne's edit took her on a hero's journey. "The million dollars, I don't really care about that," she said in an early confessional. "It's the title of Sole Survivor and the growth you get to get to that title, that's what I'm here for." Audiences watched that growth, from over-eager hopeful to underestimated threat. Still, her path to heroic glory was paved by lying and scheming, going so far as to betray her closest ally.

THE NEXT SEASON saw another shocking blindside, but this time from a castaway who played from the other end of that emotional spectrum. Father, political science Ph.D., and former gang member **Jesse Lopez**, was calm and empathetic. He had been incarcerated. He studied voting patterns professionally. He played with a strategic precision that would come to define *Survivor 43*. And Jesse had clarity in his goal. This wasn't about the experience of being on *Survivor*. It was about the money.

"I need to secure my family's future. And I'll do anything to do that," he said in a confessional. "So if I got to switch it up and be more brutal, I will."

In one of the most brutal and shocking moves in the game's recent history, the pensive Jesse Lopez blindsided his closest ally from day one, the affable Cody Assenmacher. The two had become fast friends and coconspirators, but at the final six Jesse knew: "I can't be seen as Cody's number two."

Using Cody's own idol that he had given to Jesse to build trust, and flushing another idol in the process, Jesse eliminated his happy-go-lucky partner. As Cody walked toward Jeff to have his torch snuffed, Jesse stood up and held out his hand for a shake of good will. Cody hesitated, but took it, and they embraced. The jury's jaws were agape, and at home, audiences were on the edge of their seats.

Jesse didn't win—he lost in the Final Four Fire-Making against Mike Gabler, the season's eventual winner—but he had done more than enough to establish himself as a major player in the New Era. Like the villainous tacticians of *Survivor* past, Jesse understood what it would take to win, and was willing to do whatever he needed to. Orchestrating one of the most ruthless moves in the show's later history could have made Jesse a villain, but in the New Era, audiences got more of an opportunity to understand his story and his motives.

Maryanne and Jesse each told stories that were vulnerable and nuanced, by turns empathetic and cutthroat. Through them we see how the norms around gameplay and the characters represented with increased complexity have forever complicated the monikers of heroes and villains. These were players who broke free from the archetypes—and then there were those who ignored them completely.

Carolyn Wiger

 be heard saying to a woman with long, blonde hair, wearing purple overalls, sitting between rocks on a Fijian beach.

"So, I'm just, like, talking?" she responds.

"Yeah. To me. Just pretend it's just you and I, shooting the bull," he says.

"About wha—I'm just saying who I am?" As she talks, the woman gesticulates, animated. One of her arms is tattooed with a sleeve of sunflowers. When she finishes, she scrunches her face and sticks out her tongue to the side.

"Yeah, 'I'm Carolyn. I'm a drug counselor. I'm from a suburb of the Twin Cities,'" says the producer. "Whatever you want to say, however you want to phrase it. Make sense? This is the easiest one," he adds, as the woman laughs gleefully.

This is the first thirty seconds of *Survivor 44*. Before the dramatically cut intro sequence, before the speedboats racing to the marooning, before any scramble for materials, the audience meets **Carolyn Wiger**.

In this moment, *Survivor* was showing us something we rarely see in modern *Survivor*: a player figuring out what it even means to be on the show. Carolyn was recognizing the absurdity of this situation, thinking about how to present herself to the screen. It's a small, intimate moment—just a woman asking for clarity on how to introduce herself—but it's quietly radical. Carolyn's uncertainty in this fumbling interaction is the first moment of a season in which we would watch her break down these walls of production artifice.

In recent years, *Survivor* edited contestants as if they arrived camera-ready, as fully formed characters slotted neatly into their roles. But forty-four seasons in, the show opened with a player whose first instinct was to ask: How do I do this?

From the start, a central tenet of *Survivor* has been performance. Early players wrestled with what it meant to be "yourself" on television. Richard Hatch showed that you could play a version of yourself—openly, strategically, self-aware. Jerri Manthey and Colby Donaldson became proof that the show could mint archetypes, instantly recognizable types the series would remix for years like the seductress or the all-American hero.

By the late 2000s, Tyson Apostol and Coach blew up that system entirely. They were the beginning of the end of the archetypes—players who knew they were characters and leaned into the performance. Tyson played with irony; Coach played with delusion.

Carolyn wasn't doing either.

She was not a performance of "authenticity." She's not "the weird aunt" as a role to be filled. She simply was herself—funny, frenetic, distractible, empathetic. In doing so, she brought *Survivor* somewhere it had never quite gone: to a place where authenticity and spectacle were no longer diverging paths, but, through Carolyn, connected once again.

CAROLYN GREW UP in the Twin Cities in the 1990s. "I grew up in a truly normal family," she says. Then proceeds to tell me about her dad who ran away to join the circus, and who paints mannequin heads with her for their yard displays. "Normal" is clearly a relative term for Carolyn.

She was a talkative and high-energy kid: "the weird, quirky one." Teachers told Wiger she talked too much, and the weird label followed her. "You don't know that you're different until like everyone points it out," Carolyn says. And a lot of people were pointing it out. "I thought something was wrong with me. I learned to shrink myself because I didn't fit what people wanted me to be—Is that bird dead?" Carolyn interrupts herself, looking out her window. "But I—what is that bird doing? I—What the fuck? Okay. Sorry. Wait, do birds just take naps?"

This is how conversations go with Carolyn. She is open, thoughtful, and reflective. And there are also interesting birds, laying still outside her window. But she gets back to the original subject eventually.

"So many people were telling me who I was wasn't right," Carolyn says. "I thought I had to be something different." Being made to feel self-conscious about being herself led to experimentation with drugs and alcohol, and eventually addiction. "I was getting arrested, I was transferring from school to school to school," Wiger says. "I was running from myself."

With each fresh start, Carolyn told herself that "this time it's going to be different. But that is the disease of addiction. The ability to lie to myself was scary." She has vivid memories of her dad showing up to dorms and hospital rooms "with like a frickin' sack of chicken and a big bread . . . I'll never forget the shame I felt," she says. "That will hurt me and that will haunt me."

"I couldn't look at myself in the mirror anymore," Carolyn says. That was rock bottom. "I fucking hated myself." A counselor suggested she get a calendar and mark off each sober day. Slowly the calendar filled up with days marked off. "And pretty soon I just was living," she says. She was committed to her recovery and "wanted to learn to live again, without the B.S."

Sobriety taught Wiger to lean into the things that brought her joy, to try new hobbies. She volunteered at a rabbit rescue and started gardening. "Sunflowers make me happy, so I tattooed them all over my arm. I went on a quest to, like, A: find out what I like to do, and B—well, C, D, E, F, G, H, I—to find out who I really was." Carolyn began working as a drug counselor herself, looking to help people as she was helped herself.

Carolyn also embraced the weird label. "I'm a freaky weirdo. I'm an emotional wreck. Well no, I'm an emotional *woman*," she says, correcting herself to use the language of self-love and acceptance she has worked to develop. "I held it in for a long time, so you're not gonna shut me up now."

As she continued to find herself and her passions, *Survivor* looked like the ultimate adventure. Carolyn had organized cubicle decorating contests at work, "'Cause good, I'm bringing the fun." She was deeply competitive and would go all out in those fun competitions. "We would take it to levels of, like—it should have been in a—it literally was a building. I took my cube and I made it into a house," Carolyn says. "The bird's not dead, by the way," she adds. "I just saw it moving."

A coworker, seeing the competitive verve she had for cubicle decorating, suggested she apply to *Survivor*. This final push was all she needed. Carolyn had been playing online strategy games of *Survivor* on Reddit, and she was eager for adventure. "It was out of, like, nowhere. Well, not out of nowhere because I had people at work say, 'You should apply'. And then, oh my mom, or, not my mom, my best friend, was like, 'Yeah, you should, let's go to the casting call,'" she says. She and her friend went to a casting call at a mall near the Twin Cities, but Carolyn balked at the long line: "We can't wait in line for that bullshit. I'm not waiting with these freaks." She turned around and left, but she wasn't giving up. She went home and got started on her audition tape.

In her video, "we were just fishing, and doing shit." She talked about the cubicle decorating competitions, painting mannequin heads with her dad, and addiction.

The video was, of course, deeply entertaining. She got a call right away. Casting producers were excited about her as a prospective castaway, but told her she was too "old school" and needed to watch more of the recent seasons to understand the modern game better. Carolyn wasn't a superfan; she had watched early seasons growing up and then stopped. She represented the untrained, unpolished energy the show had increasingly filtered out: "They only want superfans, which fucked up the show . . . we want a little cluelessness. Like what are your talents and what are your interests and passions and hobbies outside of just like being a fucking loser who likes the show? Oh God, Jesus, help me."

After *Winners at War* and the break for COVID, Carolyn was told (while at the vet, putting down her rabbit, "so I was already depressed") that she wasn't cast for Season 41 since there was already someone else similar to her on the cast. "Who the fuck was that?" she exclaims. But by the next round of casting for Seasons 43 and 44, Carolyn was "smooth sailing" her way to that opening scene.

Many people go onto *Survivor* to find themselves. Carolyn had already done that work in recovery. She had sat with herself and faced the parts of her she'd long tried to quiet. If *Survivor* is about stripping people down, Carolyn arrived already stripped bare. What was left was a person who had learned to live in the mess—and to find the beauty in it.

The start of Carolyn's *Survivor* journey was messy. In the very first challenge, her tribe was significantly ahead, having finished a puzzle quickly.[37] Carolyn was one of three players who had to throw a ring up and over a pole. She started with a big lead and began throwing, and throwing, and throwing, and shrieking. She took off her pants in case they were slowing her down. The other tribes passed her, often getting the ring over in one toss, while Carolyn's attempts continued to fall just short. In the end, she lost her team the challenge. She cried.

Carolyn would do a lot of crying and a lot of shrieking over the course of her *Survivor* game. She would play with her heart on her sleeve and her "freak flag flying." When her closest ally, Yam Yam Arocho—who would go on to win the season—returned from a

---

37. Carson Garrett, on Carolyn's Tika Tribe, was a NASA Engineering student and superfan who famously 3D-printed several versions of common *Survivor* puzzles to practice ahead of time.

Reward where he got to eat, she had him burp into her mouth. "I wanted to smell chocolate!" While searching for a key to the hidden idol, she compared it to digging through her son's shit after he had swallowed a tooth, so he had something to give the tooth fairy. She made faces and noises and never held back.

But Wiger's big emotions and embrace of the weird didn't mean she wasn't strategic. She found that idol and successfully planted a fake. She wiggled her way out of outsider status and became part of a core alliance—with Yam Yam and Carson Garrett—that orchestrated blindsides and ultimately defined that season's game. Carolyn wasn't one of those players where under the performance of a weirdo, a cutthroat strategist was secretly pulling the strings. Her emotion was her strategy *and* her performance.

"I had this dream to just be completely myself in a game where everyone's just like a fucking robot," Wiger says. There was zero separation or "personality compartmentalization" between the Carolyn of *Survivor* and the Carolyn of the real world. Putting your authentic self into this ruthless game can hurt in real ways. "Any trauma you've worked through, it's there. It's back. It all comes out," Carolyn says. Betrayals in the game bring back betrayals from life. Criticism of your character is really just criticism of yourself.

"You go out there and be yourself and get made fun of for it," Wiger says. "And then people gaslight you and tell you that we're just playing a game. This isn't a game. This is me and this is my life. And so when you make fun of me, when you leave me out, it is very personal to me. Fuck off."

"God, I need to research that bird," she adds.

For many players, the space between self and character on *Survivor* has become a necessary distance to play this ruthless game. Carolyn played without that armor.

In that opening scene where she was engaging directly with the producer, Wiger pulled back one layer of production and performance. She was a force that said, maybe this game didn't need to be so "game-bot-y". For Carolyn, *Survivor* was a test of strategy, yes—but also of self-compassion. Every rejection echoed something old. Every connection felt like proof that she wasn't, after all, too much.

Carolyn made it to Final Tribal where she ultimately lost to her ally, Yam Yam, as a zero-vote finalist. For this jury, her radical authenticity wasn't what they sought to reward. But for the audience, it was. Fans flooded her with messages: addicts in recovery, moms who felt invisible, kids who'd been told they were "too much."

Frannie Marin, a fellow contestant, told her at Final Tribal: "Genuinely, you have changed my life. . . . The way you are unabashedly yourself and so open and so willing to just be you changed my understanding of how I move through the world and how I tell my story."

Carolyn was awarded $100,000 from Sia—which had taken the place of the fan favorite prize in this "budget era" for production—for her authenticity and openness about addiction.[38] She now turns a significant profit from the thousands of Cameo requests that flood her inbox. Carolyn became the first New Era player to appear on Peacock's *The Traitors*, solidifying her place in reality TV legend. Other past *Survivor* players who have appeared on the show reads like a list of the game's greats: Cirie Fields, Sandra Diaz-Twine, Parvati Shallow, Boston Rob, Tony Vlachos, Jeremy Collins. Carolyn stood among them and outlasted her fellow *Survivor* alums on her season.

Carolyn's *Survivor* authenticity unlocked a new stage of her life, not just financially, but one where she felt validated in her unabashed weirdness. She was celebrated for being herself—a self that, for many years, she hated and tried to dim.

But even the love borne from this authentic way of presenting comes with complications. When you're as open as Carolyn is, many enthusiastically reciprocate that openness. Fan interactions can

38. The award was announced on a *RHAP* episode, given that live reunions became a thing of the past in the New Era.

quickly become "trauma therapy," difficult for someone as empathetic as Carolyn.

"If I see a bird who might be dead down there, I'm worried about it," she says. "If someone else is sad, I'm sad too." Carolyn knows what it is like to not want to celebrate yourself for who you are, and what it is like to be celebrated for who you are. "I truly love the freaks. I love the weirdos. I love the ones who are different. Because that's me. I can relate . . . So if I can just shout that from the rooftop, I'm going to," Wiger says. "But I also know I can't save everyone."

She's still learning that balance—between self-expression and self-protection, between the performer and the person. "I've never been good with the middle ground," she says. She has turned to fellow players, Sandra and Parvati, who have helped her search for balance between work and motherhood, between fame and self-love. They've helped her learn, "It's okay to be a woman, a mom, and do stuff and work."

"Never in a million years," Carolyn says, did she expect playing *Survivor* to bring her this kind of attention, that her authenticity could become her livelihood. There are challenges to her new recognition that she continues to work through. But in playing this radically un-performed game, Carolyn didn't just change her own life, but also the shape of the show.[39]

Performance has evolved on *Survivor.* Over time, with the turn to characters and superfans, in a world of social media and asks to return, much of the game became about carefully crafted self-presentation. Players would guess at the music that might play under their big moves and joke about what their storyline might be, referencing notorious edits from previous seasons. Carolyn made a case for stripping it all back, a case against the "gamebot-ification" of the

---

39. Despite overwhelming popularity, Carolyn was left out of the *Survivor 50* cast—an omission that shocked many.

show. Her performance was about self-acceptance, a case to show up and be yourself.

Forty-four seasons into a show, it is rare to see something new, but Carolyn represented a new turn in the evolution of performance. She has made way for more authentic weirdos in the cast. She offered an alternative path to success. You can separate your true self from the game to present as an archetype or ease the sting of a ruthless strategy, and maybe win. Or you can play fully as yourself, and hope that that's enough. In Carolyn's case, it won her love far beyond the game.

Kyle Fraser & Kamilla Karthigesu

ACROSS FIFTY SEASONS OF SHIFTING STRATEGY, PERFORMANCE, and representation, one thing on *Survivor* never changed: *connection* remained the surest path to success. Richard Hatch understood this at the beginning of this big experiment at the turn of the century, when he pulled together his ragtag Tagi Four. In the game, connections exist in many forms. Players make alliances and keep an eye out for one another; juries feel drawn to reward a particular story; players call back to the legends of yore who inspired them, intent on building upon the games their heroes played. And beyond the television screen, connections are how a character wins over an audience.

Connections are most often built on similarities, finding familiarity in a game of uncertainty. In a "game of society," we are drawn to those who reflect our own corners of it. Sue Hawk knew it long ago: "America is built on alliances. . . . Don't tell me there ain't alliances." We've seen the depth and limits of the cop connection, the loyalty to a player who reminds you of your mom, and the mutineers who "just had better bonds" on their all-white tribe.

ON SEASON 48, *Survivor* gave us one of its greatest stories of connection: the story of **Kyle Fraser** and **Kamilla Karthigesu.**

In pregame interviews, Kyle—whose relationship with *Survivor* began as a COVID binger—highlighted that his game was going to be people-focused, all about engaging with his fellow players. He was eager to find common ground, foundation on which to build a bond.

Kamilla, a long-time *Survivor* fan, didn't discuss a strategy focused on the other castaways. She called out her inspiration from players past, a connection with the lineage upon which she hoped to build. She mentioned players like Natalie Anderson (page 170) who showed her someone who looked like her could play *Survivor*. She connected with Season 41 winner Erika Casupanan, a fellow "short . . . and childish" Canadian who was initially overlooked, but who ended the season as Sole Survivor, with strategic gameplay and a strong social game. Kamilla found permission to be herself in Carolyn Wiger's (page 195) wackiness.

"When I initially saw her, I was like, oh, this lady is crazy," says Karthigesu. "But in all of her confessionals, the way she laid out what was happening, I'm like, 'This is my exact thought process. Am I the crazy lady?'"

These very different games, drawing on very different sources of inspiration, stem from the fact that Kyle and Kamilla are very different people. For Kyle, a social game would come naturally. The Virginia native quotes comedian Dave Chappelle—"My parents did just well enough so that I could grow up poor around white people"—to describe his upbringing. He knew how to build bonds both on the lacrosse team of his private school and at the Black church. A former college athlete, Kyle is now based in Brooklyn, New York, and working as an attorney. He is quick to share a smile and gives golden boy energy.

Kamilla, on the other hand, is a self-described "hater." A Canadian-born South Asian software engineer based in California, she is a fan of video games and sarcasm. "My game plan this entire time has been making people look worse than me and throwing people under the bus," she explained in a confessional before one of her many deliciously devious moves.

In pre-season "first impressions" interviews with *Entertainment Weekly*, many players noticed Fraser, pointing out his strength or saying he seemed friendly. Only one player noted Karthigesu: "The Indian girl—I like how considerate she is."

———

BOTH PLAYERS WERE approaching the game differently, but looking for the same thing: someone who saw this game the way they did.

Kamilla and Kyle started together on the Civa Tribe, and their early days played out as you might expect. Kyle hit the island with a smile, quick and eager to find that stepping stone toward connection with every player, be it sports, anime, transcendentalism. Kamilla was initially shyer around camp. She bemoaned she was on a tribe with "Disney Adults" and stayed in the background.

Soon, Kyle and Kamilla found their stepping stones to each other. While the players discussed their favorite movies, Kamilla said hers was *Holes*.

"No freaking way! No way! I was about to say *Holes!*" Kyle responded, jumping with enthusiasm. "I swear to God." This was genuine. Both of them also shared the same second-favorite movie: *The Departed*.

Later, while chatting at the water well, Kyle mentioned he was Guyanese. "I'm half Guyanese," Kamilla chimed in, animated. They both had family living in the Bronx. "I'm so happy to have something in common with someone out here," Kamilla later added in a confessional.

It wasn't much—a movie, a country, a laugh—but on *Survivor,* a little overlap can be everything. Familiarity is the fastest route to trust. "I think Kamilla's gonna be a very strategic player, and I think she's gonna know when to strike and when to pull back. And I like that. I need that around me," Kyle said in a confessional.

With this foundation, Fraser and Karthigesu would build a deep undercover alliance and soon prove to have a lethal connection.

During an idol search, Kamilla distracted their tribemates while Kyle searched with stunt performer David Kinne. Kyle eventually found the idol, leading to David whooping in excitement— the rookie move meant they needed an excuse for sound. As Kyle headed back toward the shelter, he planned on telling the others that they had found cassava, the root that grew on the Fijian island. He returned to tell his lie, but the others weren't surprised: Kamilla had already told them the same thing—randomly coming up with the same excuse. This season's idol was encased in a cryptogram, which Kyle quickly handed off to Kamilla to solve.

Later, after a randomly assigned tribe swap, the pair found themselves together again, but outnumbered. The two of them were up against a tight alliance of three calling themselves the California Girls: Joe Hunter, a lovable, brawny fire captain; Shauhin Davari, a formidable debate professor; and Thomas Krottinger, a mustachioed music executive (all of whom, as the name implies, originally bonded because they hail from the Golden State).

This new-formed tribe had lost the Immunity Challenge that day and had a date with Jeff Probst at Tribal Council that night. Back at camp, everyone agreed to have individual conversations. Kamilla walked off toward the beach with Thomas; Kyle stayed back at the shelter with Shauhin. The two of them had no time to make a plan together, but they didn't need it—their minds were already at the same place. The best path forward, they both recognized intuitively, was to play down their relationship. When talking to the California Girls, each offered to vote for the other, playing up the "anyone but me" angle that Sandra Diaz-Twine pioneered (page 61).

"Kyle said that y'all weren't close," Shauhin told Kamilla during their one-on-one. "Which unless you guys are super good actors— which is like, respect—I kind of see that." (They were, in fact, super good actors.)

The California Girls were confident—they didn't need to split the vote or be wary of any duplicity here, it seemed. Their majority alliance would stick together, and it would be a straightforward vote to eliminate either of the expendable former Civa members.

When it was finally their brief turn to talk, Karthigesu and Fraser decided on a target: Thomas. Kamilla had earned an Extra Vote in a solo mini-game the day before which she gave to Kyle. Before the votes were read, Kyle played his idol on himself (they suspected he would be the California Girls' target after Kamilla witnessed Shauhin and Thomas searching through Kyle's bag for an advantage). The California Girls' votes, all on Kyle, were negated, successfully. Kyle and Kamilla sent Thomas home to the disbelief of their tribemates. They pulled off one of the great underdog moves on the show.

EVEN AFTER THIS "master class in deception"—as the following episode is titled—Kamilla and Kyle were able to bond with their remaining new tribemates. Over a Reward the next day—pastries back at camp—the players talked about their motivations in the game. It was hard out there, but Kamilla reminded herself her father had it much harder during the Sri Lankan Civil War. "That's what keeps me going," she said. Shauhin agreed. His parents were refugees during the Iranian revolution. Joe shared that his dad came from a family of sharecroppers, and his parents were in an interracial relationship in Jim Crow-era America. Kyle was in an interracial relationship of his own.

"At the last Tribal Council . . . we were two completely different groups of people going at it," Kamilla said in a confessional. "After that shared meal today, all those struggles sort of bond us together. Oh man," she added, wiping tears from her eyes. "I don't want to vote them out." Connections in *Survivor* are often strategic, but sometimes bonds feel more real.

Luckily for Kamilla, she wouldn't have to break those bonds for a while. Her tribe won the next Immunity Challenge, and all four players made it past the merge and deep into the game. Kamilla and Kyle continued to keep their loyalty under the radar. In the post-merge game, Kyle was a core member of the majority alliance, and Kamilla was his eyes and ears on the outside. Unlike many of the dominant duos *Survivor* has seen (a cuddly Rob Mariano and Amber Brkich, an only slightly less cuddly J.T. Thomas and Stephen Fishbach), Kyle and Kamilla didn't spend a lot of time together on the island. They played their own games, knowing that with a few words, in a quick huddle up, they could be on the same page.

This strategy got them to the final four, where both realized their best shot at the win wasn't against each other. Kyle won the final Immunity Challenge and chose to bring Joe with him to the finale; he sent Kamilla to the Final Four Fire-Making, where she lost. On the jury, she was his biggest advocate, setting him up to highlight his impressive, secretive strategic game. Kyle won, in a 5-2-1 vote.

KYLE AND KAMILLA are very different people, but together on *Survivor* they were an unstoppable force. They found their stepping stones—a shared love of the same movies and video games, a common identity—and used those to build a connection and an alliance. But there was also something deeper there: a shared mind. Their ability to trust and understand the other completely, to get onto the same page, instantaneously.

A shared Guyanese heritage alone can't be credited for that mental connection. (And given the diversity of that small, South American country, there are many different experiences—Kyle is of Afro-Guyanese heritage, while Kamilla has Indo-Guyanese heritage.) Still, a shared cultural understanding brings context to their experiences. Both have older brothers, both are financial providers for their families, and both understand the sacrifices of an immigrant parent. Playing vastly different games, they found a partner who looked at the game—and perhaps the world—through a similar lens.

Survivor, at its core, is a game about connection. And those facets of identity players enter with—their life and their lens—shape those connections. Some connect despite their different stories—Rudy Boesch didn't approve of Richard Hatch's sexuality, but was impressed by his work ethic. Some connect because of familiarity—the Texan who loved his mama went to the end with the player who just so happened to be a mom with a Southern twang. Some reject the identity as a story completely—Cao Boi didn't think he fit in with the "people who are like me but not like me." Some reckon with the expectations that come with them—Sean Rector connected with Vecepia Towery most quickly because of a shared faith. But as the only Black castaways, they understood they had to play "a whole 'nother game."

For most of *Survivor*'s history, the story of these connections have been told among a largely white cast. The diversity of the New Era meant that a wider range of people had the privilege of a multi-dimensional edit. Players shared unique, textured stories of themselves. Connections were made not from a single identifier—a shared job or hometown, even race or gender—but perhaps because both your aunties might cook similar foods, or because you both know the experience of translating worlds. Differences became not just visible, but usable. For many, identity stopped being a liability or a label. It became a way in.

Kyle and Kamilla and the relationships they made show us how diversity helps connections form, and how diversity lets players author fascinating and impactful elements of their stories. They represented the diversity of the Guyanese experience: Karthigesu spoke about the atrocities of the Sri Lankan civil war, Fraser shared stories of his incarceration and of his experience with racialized policing. These weren't forced cultural conversations squeezed into the show by production, but story for the basis of connection, the most natural and essential element in this "game of society."

In its twenty-five years, *Survivor* has both shaped society and responded to it. It has soared and it has stumbled. It is flawed. But *Survivor* is at its best when it celebrates its players, when it allows them to innovate inside the game, and to play their characters fully and unabashedly. Players like Kamilla and Kyle remind us that connection isn't just how you survive—it's how the game keeps living. The players are the heart of *Survivor*, and their stories are what keeps it beating, keeps it relevant. These are their legends.

Coda: A Game in Society

AT THE MERGE OF *SURVIVOR*'S FORTY-NINE SEASON, AFTER the line that has become a *Survivor* rite of passage—"drop your buffs"—Jeff Probst framed the moment with one of his dramatic, motivating speeches:

When you talk about Survivor *greats and you think about writing your legacy, it starts at this phase of the game: the merge. Just so you know, there are spots on* Survivor 50 *that are still up for grabs. You want to be on* Survivor 50, *it happens here. This is where you make your career, or somebody makes their career off your back.*

It was the clearest he had ever articulated the stakes beyond winning: return invitations, career-making moments, the chance to write your own legacy.

Proof of *Survivor*'s legends—and the legacy new players could become a part of—was clear throughout this forty-ninth season. One player with his head on the chopping block insisted he "didn't like the way Sandra played the game," but that he would embrace an "anyone but me" mentality for the vote. (He couldn't pull it off, and was eliminated that night. Diaz-Twine, meanwhile, quickly took to social media: "Girl, bye! Queen stays Queen"). Another castaway compared a competitor's charm–disguised cunning to Parvati Shallow. A player looking to spearfish wanted "my Ozzy moment," hoping for piscatorial success. Another talked about collecting blackheads in a jar—an open-book wackiness now associated with Carolyn Wiger.

The players have always been the soul of the show; they sustain its lore and longevity. But behind Probst's fourth wall–breaking pep talk loomed the reality that Jeff is also the gatekeeper of who gets to return. A career on *Survivor* depends on playing a game production sees as worthy.

Many of the players I spoke with acknowledged this power dynamic—an economy that favors the obedient. As Sean Rector put it, "they ain't calling my Black ass anyway," which freed him to push for a more just game; he'd already felt the career-hindering consequences of speaking up. Players who hope for future opportunities may not have that same freedom.

This tension becomes especially potent as the institution behind *Survivor* shifts. Paramount, CBS's parent company, caved to the whims of the Trump administration in an effort to curry favor with the Federal Communications Commission while seeking approval for its merger with Skydance Media. CBS News settled a $16 million lawsuit with President Trump, and Paramount agreed to roll back its diversity, equity, and inclusion initiatives—including their New Era diversity promises. "I'm still shooting for having a really diverse cast because I think everybody needs to be represented," says new casting director Jesse Tannenbaum. Still, Season 50 will be the first since 2020 not to meet the 50 percent diversity threshold.

As the network rolls back its commitments to the valuable diversity it embraced a few years ago, players are responding by using their voices. During the 2025 New York City mayoral race, former castaways—including Natalie Anderson (page 170)—came together to make an ad supporting Zohran Mamdani, a candidate whose values stand in sharp contrast to those Paramount has recently embraced.

THIS POLITICAL MOMENT is not only shaping *Survivor*; it has also been shaped by it—shaped by a cultural phenomenon that spent decades warming America to showmanship and ruthlessness, to fractured performances of self increasingly untethered from truth.

Survivor 49's finale was interrupted by another Mark Burnett product: Donald Trump delivering a surprise primetime address, announced just hours before, cataloging his accomplishments. In it, facts about inflation, wages, jobs, immigration, and more seemed beyond the point—what mattered was "saying the right words," performing a story of success to the audience. An hour later, the season's finalists would give their own speeches to the jury—a propagandizing of their game, a selling of their own accomplishments.

"We're not bad people. We just play them on TV," Kelly Wiglesworth noted when she realized it was often the most duplicitous, the most manipulative, the most convincing performer, who would win the game.

From Richard to Ricard, *Survivor* has represented and reflected back how America sees morality, ambition, gender, race, and performance. Over fifty seasons, as the game has evolved, the players' stories and the ever-shifting tension of who gets to tell them remain central. Despite production's power to shape and contain those stories, it is the players—not the institution—who supply the game with its meaning. As the corporation behind the show shifts its values for the sake of profit, the players at the heart of *Survivor* continue to use their voices to assert their own values and tell their own stories. Theirs are the stories that matter.

Even in this fractured moment, *Survivor* endures—with few signs of slowing down. It could potentially air for another fifty seasons. Despite whatever political winds the network bends to, players from all walks of life will play the game, bringing their own stories and building on the show's rich lore. While *Survivor* creates a platform for these "ordinary Americans," new mediums help them amplify their voices. Their privilege of fame requires no small amount of courage. And ultimately, courage is what defines a *Survivor* legend.

Acknowledgments

I'd like to thank my parents for their Paramount+ account—and to them, my sister, my aunties, my community for their love, encouragement, and support. It takes immense privilege to write a book about a TV show while institutions crumble around us, and they've given me that.

Maya Goldfarb is a gifted editor—sharp and empathetic, precise and generous—an editor of rare instinct and deep thought. This book wouldn't be what it is without her. More importantly, she's a dear friend. After years of sitting on balconies and benches and booths, hearing me tell stories about people (read: gossip) without getting to whittle me down, I'm glad she finally got the chance. Beyond Maya, I'm deeply grateful to the extended team at Countryman Press and W. W. Norton for their support of this project.

I'm humbled (and a little ashamed) by how many talented, generous people read versions of this work and helped shape it.

I was lucky to be part of the Periplus Collective while working on this book, and luckier still to have E. Alex Jung as a mentor. Having one of this generation's great portrayers of people available to share feedback was a mind-blowing honor.

Rebecca Redelmeier and Laura Jedeed are *real* journalists doing important work that reveals injustice and shapes community. They helped me bring rigor to mine.

James Marcus—a brilliant writer and teacher—offers equal parts kindness and clarity in his notes.

Muskan Nagpal's whimsical sense of description reminds me to sometimes let my feet leave the ground and let my sentences glitter.

Elana DeSantis knows how to make complicated games feel grounded (subscribe to her NFL Substack, *Bad Sport*) with wit and coherence.

My mom, Sonia Merchant—my forever editor—is a brilliant storyteller who instilled in me the power of curiosity and faith in my own perspective.

So many friends have been encouraging, patient, and generous— talking through crises, nodding along wearily as I pontificated, allowing *Survivor* to take over too many conversations: Jaisal, Nipun, Sam, Luke, Meredith, Rosy, Dossett, Camille, McKenna, Kim, Kyle, Kiley, Emily, Maxx, Julia, Toast, Eileen, Margie, Hazel, Ossie, Michael, Ann, Janet, Babita, Arjun, Gobi and many, many more.

Sarah Sobieraj taught me that media deserves careful consideration and reflects the world it comes from.

Rob Boynton champions long, nuanced stories—and is always a generous sounding board.

So many others know much more about the *Survivor* world than I. Emily Nussbaum's work has long been a north star and her reporting on reality TV is essential. I sometimes looked to folks within the *Survivor* Reddit community for insights and fact checks, as with the unnamed admins who work tirelessly to make SurvivorWiki a fantastic resource. I consulted the work of many other journalists, influencers, podcasters and more for whom I am deeply grateful.

Finally, to the players and other figures who met with me, spoke with me, and shared their stories: It takes a leap of faith to put your story in someone else's hands. It's a privilege I don't take lightly. I'm grateful for your time, your openness, and your trust. I hope I did your rich and complicated stories justice.

Season Index

Below is a list of each season of *Survivor*, including the filming locations and the players featured in this book who played on them. Over the first thirty-two seasons, *Survivor* changed location often—each new locale representing its own challenges with environment, wildlife, and introducing new traditions. Since 2016, production has consistently taken place in Fiji.

★ Indicates season's winner

Season 5: *Survivor: Thailand* (2002)
  Location: Ko Tarutao, Satun Province, Thailand
  Featured Players: Brian Heidik★

Season 6: *Survivor: The Amazon* (2003)
  Location: Rio Negro, Amazonas, Brazil
  Featured Players: Rob Cesternino

Season 7: *Survivor: Pearl Islands—Panama* (2003)
  Location: Pearl Islands, Panama
  Featured Players: Rupert Boneham, Jonny Fairplay, Sandra Diaz-Twine★

Season 8: *Survivor: All-Stars* (2004)
  Location: Pearl Islands, Panama
  Featured Players: *Returning*—Richard Hatch, Sue Hawk, Tina Wesson, Colby Donaldson, Jerri Manthey, Ethan Zohn, Rob Mariano, Rob Cesternino, Rupert Boneham

Season 9: *Survivor: Vanuatu—Islands of Fire* (2004)
  Location: Efate, Shefa, Vanuatu
  Featured Players: N/A

Season 10: *Survivor: Palau* (2005)
  Location: Koror, Palau
  Featured Players: N/A

Season 11: *Survivor: Guatemala—The Maya Empire* (2005)
  Location: Laguna Yaxhá, Yaxhá-Nakúm-Naranjo National Park, Petén, Guatemala
  Featured Players: N/A

Season 12: *Survivor: Panama—Exile Island* (2006)
  Location: Pearl Islands, Panama
  Featured Players: Cirie Fields

Season 13: *Survivor: Cook Islands* (2006)
Location: Aitutaki, Cook Islands
Featured Players: Yul Kwon,★ Cao Boi, Ozzy Lusth, Parvati Shallow

Season 14: *Survivor: Fiji* (2007)
Location: Macuata, Vanua Levu, Fiji
Featured Players: Yau-Man Chan

Season 15: *Survivor: China* (2007)
Location: Zhelin, Jiujiang, Jiangxi, China
Featured Players: N/A

Season 16: *Survivor: Micronesia—Fans vs. Favorites* (2008)
Location: Koror, Palau
Featured Players: *Returning*—Parvati Shallow,★ Jonny Fairplay, Cirie Fields, Ozzy Lusth, Yau-Man Chan

Season 17: *Survivor: Gabon—Earth's Last Eden* (2008)
Location: Wonga-Wongue Presidential Reserve, Estuaire, Gabon
Featured Players: N/A

Season 18: *Survivor: Tocantins—The Brazilian Highlands* (2009)
Location: Jalapão, Tocantins, Brazil
Featured Players: Benjamin "Coach" Wade, Tyson Apostol, J.T. Thomas★

Season 19: *Survivor: Samoa* (2009)
Location: Upolu, Samoa
Featured Players: Russell Hantz

Season 20: *Survivor: Heroes vs. Villains* (2010)
Location: Upolu, Samoa
Featured Players: *Returning*—Colby Donaldson, Jerri Manthey, Rob Mariano, Rupert Boneham, Sandra Diaz-Twine,★ Cirie Fields, Parvati Shallow, Benjamin "Coach" Wade, Tyson Apostol, J.T. Thomas, Russell Hantz

Season 21: *Survivor: Nicaragua* (2010)
Location: San Juan del Sur, Rivas, Nicaragua
Featured Players: N/A

Season 22: *Survivor: Redemption Island* (2011)
Location: San Juan del Sur, Rivas, Nicaragua
Featured Players: *Returning*—Rob Mariano,★ Russell Hantz

Season 23: *Survivor: South Pacific* (2011)
Location: Upolu, Samoa
Featured Players: John Cochran, *Returning*—Ozzy Lusth, Benjamin "Coach" Wade

Season 24: *Survivor: One World* (2012)
Location: Upolu, Samoa
Featured Players: Kim Spradlin★

Season 25: *Survivor: Philippines* (2012)
Location: Caramoan, Camarines Sur, Philippines
Featured Players: N/A

Season 26: *Survivor: Caramoan—Fans vs. Favorites* (2013)
Location: Caramoan, Camarines Sur, Philippines
Featured Players: *Returning*—John Cochran★

Season 27: *Survivor: Blood vs. Water* (2013)
Location: Palaui Island, Santa Ana, Cagayan, Philippines
Featured Players: *Returning*—Tina Wesson, Rupert Boneham, Tyson Apostol★

Season 28: *Survivor: Cagayan—Brawn vs. Brains vs. Beauty* (2014)
Location: Palaui Island, Santa Ana, Cagayan, Philippines
Featured Players: Tony Vlachos★

Season 29: *Survivor: San Juan del Sur—Blood vs. Water* (2014)
Location: San Juan del Sur, Rivas, Nicaragua
Featured Players: Kelley Wentworth, Natalie Anderson,★ Jeremy Collins

Season 39: *Survivor: Island of the Idols* (2019)
Location: Mamanuca Islands, Fiji
Featured Players: N/A

Season 40: *Survivor: Winners at War* (2020)
Location: Mamanuca Islands, Fiji
Featured Players: *Returning*—Ethan Zohn, Rob Mariano, Sandra Diaz-Twine, Yul Kwon, Parvati Shallow, Tyson Apostol, Kim Spradlin, Natalie Anderson, Jeremy Collins, Tony Vlachos★

Season 41: *Survivor 41* (2021)
Location: Mamanuca Islands, Fiji
Featured Players: Ricard Foyé

Season 42: *Survivor 42* (2022)
Location: Mamanuca Islands, Fiji
Featured Players: Maryanne Oktech★

Season 43: *Survivor 43* (2022)
Location: Mamanuca Islands, Fiji
Featured Players: Jesse Lopez

Season 44: *Survivor 44* (2023)
Location: Mamanuca Islands, Fiji
Featured Players: Carolyn Wiger

Season 45: *Survivor 45* (2023)
Location: Mamanuca Islands, Fiji
Featured Players: N/A

Season 46: *Survivor 46* (2024)
Location: Mamanuca Islands, Fiji
Featured Players: N/A

Season 47: *Survivor 47* (2024)
Location: Mamanuca Islands, Fiji
Featured Players: N/A

Season 48: *Survivor 48* (2025)
   Location: Mamanuca Islands, Fiji
   Featured Players: Kamilla Karthigesu, Kyle Fraser★

Season 49: *Survivor 49* (2025)
   Location: Mamanuca Islands, Fiji
   Featured Players: N/A

Season 50: *Survivor 50: In the Hands of the Fans* (2026)
   Location: Mamanuca Islands, Fiji
   Featured Players: *Returning*—Colby Donaldson, Cirie Fields,
   Ozzy Lusth, Benjamin "Coach" Wade, Mike White, Kamilla
   Karthigesu, Kyle Fraser

Select Bibliography

"About Coach's Tibetan Martial Arts." Reddit, 2025.

Battan, Carrie. "Mike White on Money, Status, and Appearing on 'Survivor.'" *The New Yorker.* July 18, 2021.

Cesternino, Rob. "About Rob Cesternino." RobHasAWebsite. RHAP, November 18, 2025.

"Five facts about marrow registry diversity (and why ethnicity is the key to a perfect match)." Gift of Life, December 18, 2018.

"Kamilla Karthigesu: Survivor 48 Pre-Game Interview." YouTube. RHAP: We Know Reality TV, February 12, 2025.

Longeretta, Emily. "Jeff Probst on Worrying 'Survivor' Was 'Doomed,' Season 50 Gameplay." *Variety.* April 14, 2025.

Neal, Rome. "Hawk and Hatch: Getting Past It." CBS News, March 4, 2004.

"News Release U.S. Department of Justice." US Department of Justice, May 16, 2006.

Nussbaum, Emily. *Cue the Sun.* Random House, 2024.

Ross, Dalton. "Kamilla drops 'Survivor 48' pre-merge intel in exclusive mid-game interview." *Entertainment Weekly.* April 1, 2025.

Ross, Dalton. "'Survivor 48' cast reveal the players they want to work with and against." *Entertainment Weekly.* January 31, 2025.

Ross, Dalton. "Survivor: Kellee Kim speaks out on inappropriate touching incidents." *Entertainment Weekly.* November 19, 2019.

Ross, Dalton. "Survivor: Mike White writes the most disturbing fan fiction imaginable." *Entertainment Weekly.* May 6, 2021.

Simpson, Kaitlin. "Every 'Survivor' Contestant Who Won the Sia Award." *Us Weekly*, February 28, 2024.

"Survivor Wiki." Wiki. Accessed November 18, 2025.

"'Survivor' winner Kyle Fraser's pre-game interview." YouTube. *CBS Sunday Morning*, May 22, 2025.

"The popularity of the name Colby after Survivor." Reddit, 2018.

Wigler, Josh. "'Survivor:' Jeff Probst Speaks on Dan Spilo Controversy." Hollywood Reporter. November 13, 2019.